What a wonderful, much needed book on the topic of joy! Thank you, Kyllie, for this timely, candid telling of your 'joy journey'. In the midst of pain and health challenges, you have included us in the story of God turning your mourning into joy. This is a book that needs to go far and wide. It is a book that will undoubtedly help fill a void in many joy-deprived lives.

— **Colin Shaw**
Co-Founder of City by City, NZ
Whanganui, New Zealand

I love discovering more about joy, as it is one-third of the kingdom (Romans 14:17)! I am so thankful for Kyllie Martin and her great book, *Unlimited Joy*, which will help us go deeper into a life of gladness and cheerfulness. Kyllie shares her journey of finding joy through life's celebrations and grief process, and her encounters with the God of joy. Her testimony, insights and practical applications will equip and inspire you to access a life of growing joy. Well done, Kyllie. This is a needed and timely book. I highly recommend it.

— **Steve Backlund**
Co-Founder of Igniting Hope Ministries
Author of *Possessing Joy* and *Victorious Mindsets*

Unlimited Joy by Kyllie Martin is a very thoughtful, unique and down-to-earth gift to readers hungry to taste real, abiding, 'spilling-over' joy. Through her own family's story of heartbreak and struggle, Kyllie leads us on a journey through scripture as well as her own personal experiences to discover the abundance of joy Jesus promised His followers.

— **Bridget Hilliard**
Co-Founder of Hope Africa
Engage Pastor, Bethel Leaders Network

Kyllie Martin's book, *Unlimited Joy*, is a must-read for every follower of Christ. Kyllie takes us on the journey of joy, but she also prepares the reader for the 'Art of Lament' which is equally important in unleashing the joy of the Lord in one's life. I found the chapter on 'Joy Thieves' particularly helpful, where Kyllie shares practical points regarding our physical and emotional needs. This book draws the reader into desiring the joy of the Lord. I felt joy, I felt moved to tears, and I feel extremely grateful that Kyllie has heard from Heaven and has given us this amazing resource. A truly refreshing read!

— **Carmel Malcolm**
Pastor, Clifflife Church
Whanganui, New Zealand

Unlimited Joy brings a much-needed message for the Church: Supernatural joy is the believer's birthright—and it's readily available to us now. With a powerful testimony of having discovered the strength that joy brings firsthand, Kyllie unpacks the scriptures to move the reader from a place of intellectually knowing about the joy of the Lord to actually experiencing it. I was profoundly ministered to as I read and outworked the activations at the end of each chapter, and months later, still find myself remembering and using the practical tools that she offered. This book will cause you to pursue and encounter the fullness of joy Jesus promises us, but ultimately, the One who is joy.

— **Aimée Walker**
Founder of The Devoted Collective
Auckland, New Zealand

Unlimited JOY

Torn Curtain Publishing
Wellington, New Zealand
www.torncurtainpublishing.com

© Copyright 2023 Kyllie Martin. All rights reserved.

ISBN Softcover 978-0-473-67055-9
ISBN Hardcover 978-0-473-67056-6
ISBN EPub 978-0-473-67057-3
ISBN Audiobook 978-0-473-67058-0

No portion of this book may be reproduced, stored in a retrieval system or transmitted in any form or by any means—electronic, mechanical, photocopy, recording or otherwise—except for brief quotations in printed reviews or promotion, without prior written permission from the author.

Unless otherwise indicated, all Scripture quotations are taken from the Holy Bible, New International Version©, NIV©. Copyright ©1973, 1978, 1984, 2011 by Biblica, Inc.© Used by permission of Zondervan. All rights reserved worldwide.

Scripture quotations marked NASB are taken from the New American Standard Bible®, Copyright © 1960, 1971, 1977, 1995, 2020 by The Lockman Foundation. Used by permission. All rights reserved. lockman.org

Scripture quotations marked ESV are from The ESV© Bible (The Holy Bible, English Standard Version©), copyright © 2001 by Crossway, a publishing ministry of Good News Publishers. Used by permission. All rights reserved.

Scripture quotations marked AMP are taken from the Amplified Bible, Copyright © 1954, 1958, 1962, 1964, 1965, 1987 by The Lockman Foundation. Used by permission.

Scripture quotations marked MSG or "The Message" are taken from The Message. Copyright 1993, 1994, 1995, 1996, 2000, 2001, 2002. Used by permission of NavPress Publishing Group. http://www.navpress.com/

Scripture quotations marked BSB are taken from The Holy Bible, Berean Study Bible, BSB. Copyright ©2016, 2018 by Bible Hub. Used by Permission. All Rights Reserved Worldwide. www.berean.bible

Scripture quotations marked KJV are taken from The Authorized (King James) Version. Rights in the Authorized Version in the United Kingdom are vested in the Crown. Reproduced by permission of the Crown's patentee, Cambridge University Press.

Scripture quotations marked CEB are from the COMMON ENGLISH BIBLE. © Copyright 2011 COMMON ENGLISH BIBLE. All rights reserved. Used by permission. (www.CommonEnglishBible.com).

Scripture quotations marked CSB have been taken from the Christian Standard Bible®, Copyright © 2017 by Holman Bible Publishers. Used by permission. Christian Standard Bible® and CSB® are federally registered trademarks of Holman Bible Publishers.

Cover image by Vitaly Korovin. Used with permission.

Cataloguing in Publishing Data
  Title: Unlimited Joy: Accessing All That Is Promised
  Author: Kyllie Martin
  Subjects: Christian living; Death, Grief & Bereavement; Personal Growth; Biblical Studies; Spiritual Growth; Pastoral Resources

A copy of this title is held at the National Library of New Zealand.

Unlimited JOY

KYLLIE MARTIN

In loving memory of Boaz and Daniel. We lost you far too soon, yet your lives brought such value and joy.

Foreword

What a pleasure it is to be asked to write the foreword for *Unlimited Joy*. Writing forewords for authors who I know (who are actually walking in what they teach) is one of the delights of my life. Having watched Kyllie's journey over the past several years while we were both living in Redding, California for a season and since my return to New Zealand, I can with all honesty say that Kyllie is the real deal. She walks the talk!

Reading through *Unlimited Joy* there was such a refreshing happening in my heart as I absorbed each word, page, and chapter. The connection that most believers miss in life is the reality that joy should not be controlled by external circumstances but is in fact an 'inside job'. Our joy is not circumstance-based; our joy is because we have Jesus!

This is an incredible book that will not only encourage believers in Christ as they digest each word but bring them back into alignment with the person of Jesus as they are hit with truth after truth.

The Bible tells us that Jesus Himself was full of joy more than all His companions (Hebrews 1:9), as was prophesied in Psalm 45:7. Joy is more than a precious commodity; it is a person, and His name is Jesus. We are told in 1 John 4:17 that as He is, so are we in this world. Jesus was filled with joy more than His companions, so should we be too, since we have the person of joy living inside each of us!

I highly encourage you to do yourself a favor and make an investment in yourself—take the time to read *Unlimited Joy*, and let your life become a fountain of bubbling-up joy to a world that so needs an outbreak of joy.

Well done, Kyllie. I'm so very proud of this wonderful achievement and look forward to having the finished product in my hands so I can feast again over and over on truth!

— **Chris Gore**
Founder, Release the Healers New Zealand
Author of *Walking in Supernatural Healing Power*,
Apprehended Identity, and *Positioned*
www.chrisgore.org

Contents

Foreword

Chapter 1	*Joy Unexpected*	1
Chapter 2	*The Promise of Joy*	11
Chapter 3	*The Person of Joy*	23
Chapter 4	*The Position of Joy*	33
Chapter 5	*Joy Overflowing*	43
Chapter 6	*Joy and Trust*	51
Chapter 7	*Joy for Mourning*	63
Chapter 8	*Sowing in Tears*	73
Chapter 9	*A Pathway Back to Joy*	83
Chapter 10	*The Banquet Table*	97
Chapter 11	*Shouting for Joy*	109
Chapter 12	*Joy Thieves*	119
Chapter 13	*Joy, Our Strength*	131
Chapter 14	*The Restoring Power of Joy*	139

An Impartation of Joy   147

Author's Note   149

Acknowledgements   153

CHAPTER ONE

Joy Unexpected

These things I have spoken to you so that My joy may be in you, and that your joy may be made full.
John 15:11 NASB

From the balcony of the auditorium I was perfectly positioned to see everything that was happening below. We were participating in corporate worship when, out of the corner of my eye, I noticed a young man knock over his coffee cup, liquid spilling all over the floor and extending out for meters in every direction. Flustered, he scrambled around trying to figure out what to do before rushing out of the room to find someone to help clean it up.

I wouldn't have thought anything more of the incident, except that when I turned my focus back to worship, I sensed the quiet prompting of the Holy Spirit to "take note." I stopped briefly, thinking to myself, *What's a cup of coffee got to do with anything?*

Just then the band launched into another song. It was one I recognized from my childhood, one we had sung in Sunday School about the joy being down in our hearts to stay. "Noooo!" I heard the Holy Spirit cry louder and clearer than I had ever heard Him before. "I don't want My joy to stay down in your heart, I want it overflowing and spilling out all over the place, just like that cup of coffee!"

UNLIMITED JOY

Only a week prior to this, I had been asking the Lord for more of His joy in my life. Much of the past twenty years had been difficult, but I thought I had navigated them well—joyfully even. It wasn't until I arrived in Redding and observed the leaders at the Bethel School of Supernatural Ministry—many of whom were carrying heavy burdens in their personal lives, yet still evidenced the joy of the Lord—that I recognized how little joy I truly felt. There was something different about these people.

I had always struggled with people who were 'fake', and could discern when people were acting, but that didn't seem to be the case here; the joy I was witnessing felt genuine and authentic. And it was infectious! These people each carried joy in a different way. Some were exuberant, while others were childlike in nature—even the introverts were cheerful. After only a few weeks of being in this environment I could tell that they had something I lacked. Something that I wanted. That's when I started asking the Lord to teach me about the joy I was seeing.

As I continued to worship that day, a phrase kept going through my head, as if on repeat: *everlasting to everlasting, everlasting to everlasting, everlasting to everlasting*... honestly, it was starting to get distracting. I felt my body move rhythmically with the music in the shape of an infinity sign. This, too, was rather distracting. I began to get frustrated, and I was not shy in telling God so!

"Yes, Lord, I know you are *everlasting to everlasting*. You're infinite, that's true, but can I get back to worship now?" That was, after all, why I was there.

But God was trying to tell me something, and I obviously wasn't listening close enough because as I continued to sing I began to feel a weird sensation, as if warm liquid was running down my left leg and then my right, like I was wetting my pants. Panic leapt in my chest, and my brain struggled to register what was going on as thoughts raced through my mind. *What?! How embarrassing! How did this happen? I didn't cough or sneeze, I wasn't jumping up and down or anything.* Plenty of women have incontinence issues, but it had never been a problem for me, even after the birth of my children, and definitely not during worship. I wondered if anyone had noticed. Could I leave discreetly without being seen?

I ran my hands up and down my jeans. Thankfully, they still felt dry. I opened my eyes and quickly glanced down, but saw no evidence of liquid. Perplexed, I shook my head and returned to worshiping, but the sensation of leaking urine started again. By now I knew this must be the Holy Spirit speaking to me, even if I didn't fully understand. *What was He trying to say?*

I love the Lord's sense of humor, and how the Holy Spirit speaks to us in ways He knows we will grasp—eventually, at least. As a physical therapist, I knew the common causes and treatments of urinary incontinence, but I wanted to explore what this sensation symbolized, so I stopped singing, centered myself on the Holy Spirit, and asked Him, "What are you trying to say?", to which He quietly replied, "My joy is everlasting, infinite. I don't want it to stay down in your heart! I want it spilling over in all directions and leaking from you uncontrollably!"

Just then, pockets of laughter broke out and seemed to spread across the room. As I turned my attention to it, I felt laughter bubble up from deep within me. It was neither loud nor obtrusive, but gentle, freeing. I turned and looked at my husband. He seemed surprised to hear me laugh. This was not the norm for me—I hardly ever laughed out loud. In fact, I had always said I "laughed on the inside." As we stared at each other, Lincoln started to chuckle gently too. We had been through so much together it often felt like we just moved from one trial to the next. After all the years of struggle and tears, it warmed my heart to see him laugh. I was excited to be sharing this moment with him, and hope began to enter my heart for the future.

A JOURNEY OF DISCOVERY

Let me say it before you do—that experience was weird, I agree! While I'd had visions and encounters with the Holy Spirit before, this was like nothing I had ever experienced. And believe me, I had questions! You probably do too. Perhaps you're thinking: *This is strange. Was that really God talking to her? Or was it just her subconscious projecting what she had been asking for onto her mind? Is it even biblical?* Perhaps that story is so outside your comfort zone you are wondering whether to read any further. If that's you, I encourage you to simply allow your questions to take you on a journey of discovery as they did for me.

Let me tell you my story . . .

For a long time, I had been extremely wary of anything too 'wacky' to do with the Holy Spirit. The very thing I engaged in that day, 'holy laughter', I had previously found offensive—I simply thought it was rude that people would disrupt a whole room of people by laughing loudly or screaming even. I had a rather conservative upbringing in the Salvation Army Church, and while I'm deeply grateful for the solid foundation in the Word this wonderful church gave me, and the heart they fostered for the lost and the suffering, there was little emphasis on the Holy Spirit. As a result, I thought that the Holy Spirit only spoke in a small, quiet voice. I was cynical of what I thought to be the more 'extreme presentations' of the Spirit—the shaking and the laughter—and I thought that anyone who was 'slain in the Spirit' had simply been pushed over by others.

The Lord knew my reluctance to explore things of the Spirit, and over the past twenty years He has taken me on a gentle journey, graciously revealing Himself to me in new ways. Through trials and tribulation, I had learnt to discern His voice. In John 10, Jesus repeatedly talks about how His sheep know His voice and they follow it. My own willingness to follow His voice was tentative at first, but as I experienced Him in new ways, my confidence grew. Slowly, He showed me that the very things I had been cynical of, were indeed of Him—well, for the most part anyway.

It was this confidence to recognize the Lord's voice that enabled me to discern it was Him speaking to me during the worship that day in the auditorium. I could see that the fruit of what I was hearing was of the Spirit: This encounter left me with a hunger to spend time with Him, to study the Word, and to seek greater understanding of what the Holy Spirit had shared with me. In all honesty, I could hardly wait to get home and unpack it all with Him!

The end of the day soon rolled around. I did my best to stay engaged with everything we needed to do as we picked up the kids and sorted snacks and homework and dinner and baths and so on, but inside, my desperation to process the day's events with the Lord was growing. Finally, after what felt like an eternity, I excused myself from my husband and went into my room to do some research and seek God about what had taken place during worship that day.

I began by looking up the definition of 'everlasting' and found it meant, 'eternity, lasting or enduring through all time, tediously persistent'. *Wow!* No wonder my body was being moved by the Spirit in an infinity sign! I dug a little deeper and did a search of Scriptures containing the phrase, "everlasting to everlasting." Psalm 90:1-2 caught my attention:

Lord, you have been our dwelling place throughout all generations.
Before the mountains were born or you brought forth the whole world,
from everlasting to everlasting you are God.

My next search took me deeper still. I added joy to the mix, and found Isaiah 51:11:

Those the Lord has rescued will return. They will enter Zion with
singing; everlasting joy will crown their heads. Gladness and joy will
overtake them, and sorrow and sighing will flee away.

As I read these Scriptures, a hunger grew in me to experience that type of joy—to know everlasting, eternal joy that endures throughout a lifetime and beyond. A smile came to my face, and I began to speak to God: "How tediously persistent you have been in my life! Oh Lord, if only I could have had tediously persistent joy through struggles." Then I prayed, "Lord crown me with everlasting joy! I want to be overtaken with gladness so that sorrow and sighing will flee."

I had endured enough sorrow to last me a lifetime; I was ready to know joy.

POSITIONING OURSELVES FOR THE 'MORE' OF GOD

Lincoln and I had been Christians and followed the Lord for decades, but there came a point where we were dissatisfied with just 'churchgoing' on a Sunday and the often-powerless Christianity we had been experiencing. For more than fifteen years we had been praying for healing for my husband without seeing it come to fruition—well not yet, anyway—and this had created a deep longing within us for *more*.

When the Lord called us to leave our home in Whanganui, a small city in New Zealand, and move with our two children to Redding, California to attend a ministry school that focused on healing and the supernatural power of God, it felt like He was taking us into the 'more' we were hungering for. He generously confirmed this call through six different sources—and it would turn out that we would need all six to keep our resolve to go!

We started the process of getting visas and preparing for an international move, but smack bang in the middle of it, the Covid-19 pandemic hit, and New Zealand went into 'shut-down' along with the rest of the world. The fear of Covid was immense, and the risk of it overwhelming our small country's health system, with only two-hundred-and-fifty intensive care beds in total, was a very real possibility. The government acted hard and fast in response, enforcing a nationwide lock-down, the goal being total elimination of the virus in New Zealand. Schools, workplaces, shops and eateries were all closed for an initial period of eight weeks. Only essential services such as doctors and supermarkets were allowed to remain open. Sadly, the embassy wasn't considered essential, and all issuing of visas stopped. With no certainty on when anything would reopen, it looked like our trip was on hold indefinitely.

As time ticked on, we felt that we needed to stay in faith—to keep believing in what we couldn't yet see. God had never confirmed anything in our lives more clearly than going to ministry school, so we knew we had to do everything we could to get there. In faith, we completed our visa paperwork declaring the doors would be open. In faith, we resigned from our jobs. And in faith, we decluttered our house and garage—quite the feat after twelve years of living there! We worked out the latest date we could leave New Zealand if the kids were to be able to start the school year in America. As the weeks went by, I felt like Gideon starting with thirty thousand men but soon dwindling to three hundred. Then we saw the Lord make a way. After nine long months, the embassy reopened, and just two weeks before we needed to leave, our visas came through—just enough time to rent out our house in New Zealand, find a house in Redding, sell the car, lease one in the States, and book our now very expensive flights!

The response from our friends and family was mixed. They were surprised that we would travel during a pandemic and were concerned for our safety, but we knew that we had to follow God's calling on our lives. As we left New Zealand, the "safest place on earth", we reassured everyone that Redding had low numbers of Covid cases, one of the lowest in the country, and we would be fine. Every student in the school had to get tested, and all were found to be negative before the school year started. Sadly, this didn't remain the case. Within a few weeks, Covid broke out in both the county and the school. The numbers were so high that after only two weeks, classes were forced to go online.

There we were, one month after arriving in the States, sitting in our rental property doing school online. Then, to top it all off, we contracted the dreaded Covid-19 virus. Yes, I know it's ironic. We had moved to attend a 'supernatural school' where students are activated in miracles and healing, and now we were suffering from Covid (fortunately we only had mild symptoms, but it was still another blow). So, there we were, having moved to the other side of the world, sick, isolated, tired, and lonely. As disappointment set in, we desperately needed the joy of the Lord to strengthen us.

JOY THROUGH A COMPUTER SCREEN

While all this was happening, I enrolled in a class called "Living in the Realm of Healing and Miracles", which ran for five weeks. I instantly loved the teacher. He was so passionate about God and spending time in His presence and the Word. But most of all, he oozed the joy of the Lord—it was as though the joy was spilling and leaking out of him. He simply couldn't contain it. He even told us a funny story about how he had been challenged by some other believers that he must be faking it, because no one is that joyful!

This teacher's joy was contagious—or more rightly I should say, the joy he carried from the Lord was contagious. Even over Zoom calls I was often hit with waves of laughter and would leave the class feeling more positive and revitalized. It was more than his upbeat personality; it was what he carried. I know it sounds bizarre to say that the joy of the Lord could be shared through a computer screen, but God is omnipotent and omnipresent. Nothing is too hard for Him. One week during the online class, I was healed of the lingering effects of Covid without even being prayed for by anyone else. I just said to the Lord, "This is getting tiring, can You heal me please?" and what had been lingering for weeks was gone within an hour. Over the next six months, as we used technology to connect with each other and the world, we found that healings via Zoom became commonplace.

During each class, I found I was being topped up with the joy my teacher possessed. As the course came to an end, I started asking God how I could increase and maintain His joy in my life without the regular interaction with my teacher. I knew I couldn't keep relying on what others had and were prepared to give me—I needed it for myself. This request took me on a journey of seeking after joy, seeking after the One who is fullness of joy. This book is the outpouring of that pursuit.

Today, those around me can see the difference joy has made in my life. I laugh louder and more often, and am more childlike in nature, than ever before. The truth is, joy has fundamentally changed how I behave. But more than that, as joy 'leaks out', I have seen atmospheres shift and dynamics be transformed in my own family—and beyond.

Imagine if we all became conduits of heaven's joy! I have discovered this is indeed possible. For me, the first step was acknowledging that joy was fundamentally lacking in my life, then realizing that fullness of joy is available to us today, and simply choosing to ask for it. This is where your journey starts too.

ACTIVATION

Sit with the Lord and set your heart and mind on the Holy Spirit, the Source of joy. Share your thoughts, feelings, needs and desires about joy, as well as your reservations and concerns. Use the following prompts to help you dig deeper in the conversation:

1. Do you need or want more joy in your life? Why?

2. In what parts of your life do you feel joy is lacking? Where do you most want to see change?

3. Have you been cynical about holy laughter and other more demonstrative expressions of the Spirit's work? Why or why not?

4. What will convince you that your joy levels are different? Start asking Him to give you more joy!

CHAPTER TWO

The Promise of Joy

The expectations of the righteous result in joy.
Proverbs 10:28 CEB

I met my husband, Lincoln, shortly after graduating from university with a degree in physiotherapy. We were living in Wellington, the capital of New Zealand, at the time, and were introduced by mutual friends. I was instantly drawn to his trendy style and outgoing nature (which helped make up for the fact that I was more reserved and introverted). By date number four, I knew that I wanted to marry this man and share the rest of my life with him.

The first few months of dating were a whirlwind of emotions and romance; it was as though I was living in a dream. Unbeknown to us, that happiness wouldn't last. At Easter, just four months into our relationship, my father was diagnosed with inoperable metastatic melanoma and given only weeks to months to live. Wanting to support my mum and be there for my dad's last days, I made the decision to move back to my home city of Hamilton, seven hours' drive away. But my heart was still in Wellington, and soon I found myself grieving not only my dad's prognosis, but also the loss of my old life. What had started as a series of joy-filled dates now became one of sad long-distance calls interspersed with the occasional visit, but I was consumed by my dad's sickness, and even these were difficult for me to enjoy.

It was my birthday just a few weeks after I returned to Hamilton, and Lincoln told all our friends that he was going to surprise me by proposing. Lincoln did the honorable thing, asking my dad for permission, but despite his best efforts, the night didn't quite play out as he envisioned—Lincoln ended up enduring three hours of repetitive questioning from my dad, who by now was in a drug-induced haze. In the meantime, I had taken myself off to bed, feeling ill from the stress.

The proposal later that evening was probably the least romantic thing you could imagine. Picture me lying in bed, with Lincoln crouching at my side, completely oblivious to the fact that he was trying to propose as he poured out his heart, telling me he loved me and wanted to spend the rest of his life with me. "Yes, but there's no hurry," I distractedly replied—not the response the poor guy was expecting! Undeterred, he pulled out an engagement ring and asked me to marry him.

I was shocked and disappointed. It wasn't that I didn't want to marry him, but *right now? Like this?* A proposal was meant to be the pinnacle of romance, and there I was, sick in bed, with no grand gesture to mark the occasion. I didn't say anything, but internally I mourned. Then I felt selfish for feeling this way. After all, it was nothing compared to what my mum was going through. But I couldn't help it, and the feelings of loss were magnified when couples all around us were announcing their own engagements and sharing their romantic proposal stories.

Two weeks later, my father, at the young age of fifty-two, quietly passed away in his sleep. For the next six months I continued to live at home, supporting my mum and doing my best to plan a wedding under the cloud of grief. In spite of everything, we made it through, and in the end, our wedding day was stunning—the sun shone, the sky was a deep blue, there was not a cloud in sight. I stepped out of the bridal car, and my mum walked me into the church and down the aisle to a weeping Lincoln, the emotional one of the two in our relationship.

THE PROMISE OF JOY

DIFFICULT BEGINNINGS

Not long after our wedding, I was diagnosed with endometriosis. Looking back, I could see that my symptoms had been slowly creeping in over the past year, probably exacerbated by the stress and grief. But the slow creep was over, and for the following two years I was hit full-force by this illness, suffering pelvic and back pain, gastric problems, and extreme fatigue. Eventually I underwent several surgeries. As a previously healthy, active twenty-five-year-old, none of this was what I had expected. Nor was it how I had foreseen our first few years of married life.

As my health started to improve, we began planning our 'OE'—an 'overseas excursion', which is a rite of passage for many young New Zealanders. We decided to spend a year in the United Kingdom where locum physical therapists were being paid extremely well, before going on to do a Discipleship Training School with YWAM on their 'Mercy Ships'. We completed all the visa paperwork and booked our flights, but needed to show $10,000 in our bank account before our visa could be approved. To save money for this, we moved in with Lincoln's parents for three months. We had only been with them a few days when, while walking to the video store (yes, way back then, when video stores were still a thing!), Lincoln stumbled over a crack in the pavement, jarring his back which sent excruciating pain down his legs. Unable to call for help (back then, cellphones were not routinely carried either!), we struggled through the ten-minute walk home with Lincoln leaning all his weight heavily on me, every step causing him to wince in pain.

When Lincoln was thirteen, he had broken his spine in an accident and had his vertebrae fused two years later. At the emergency department that day, and in subsequent specialist appointments, the medical staff found that the spinal fusion was now unstable. At the age of twenty-eight, Lincoln was told he had arthritis; he had the back of a seventy-year-old man.

This new injury resulted in a lot of change in our lives. With our OE no longer possible and Lincoln unable to work, he decided to make the most of a bad situation and enrolled to do his social work studies, something he had been talking about since we had been married. We felt God prompt us to move to Whanganui, a smaller city where there was a senior physical therapy job in my specialty. But not long after we moved there, Lincoln's back worsened when one disc prolapsed and another tore. What followed was the worst time of our lives: Over an eighteen-month period Lincoln was admitted to hospital twelve times and put on a cocktail of hard pain killers. With my husband in a medicated daze, I was left feeling isolated. After only half a semester, he pulled out of his studies, unable to sit or concentrate long enough to cope.

For the next four years, Lincoln was on a disability allowance, living in severe pain and largely immobile, having to rely on crutches and a walking frame to get around. He was depressed and hopeless. We lived from doctor's appointment to doctor's appointment, and outings were limited. When we did manage to get out, it usually revolved around food, which resulted in significant weight gain for both of us, only exacerbating the sadness we felt. Even going to church was hard—we had to choose between staying either for the worship or the message, because Lincoln couldn't tolerate sitting through both.

It was painful watching all our 'couple-friends' move on with their lives, building great careers, leading physically active lifestyles, heading overseas for trips, and starting their families when we could barely make love. Our twenties were supposed to be some of the best years of our lives, and here we were just watching ours slip away. Compounding things was the fact that my 'fantastic' new job was not so fantastic. Our department was chronically understaffed, and the manager had no vision or interest in change. It was difficult having to go to work day after day and care for other people, then head home to do the same for my husband. I was tired, worn out, stressed, and losing hope.

This led to a crisis of faith. I questioned where God was in this situation; we were willing to serve Him, yet nothing in our lives was going 'right'. Nothing was as I had imagined, and I felt ripped off. *If God is truly good, why was this happening?* But God did not let us down, and as I wrestled through my questions, I found Him to be good and faithful—even in our suffering. We encountered His love in such tangible ways and saw Him do the miraculous so many times that I could no longer question His character. Now I truly know that God is good.

After two surgeries, Lincoln's back improved enough to return to work part-time. God came through once again, opening doors for a job Lincoln was underqualified for and enabling him to complete his social work degree with the provision of a scholarship. But while we were grateful for these gains, behind the scenes we were struggling to start a family. Everyone around us was having children, and once again, we felt left behind and hopeless. I remember one eight-week period where eight couples shared with us the news that they were expecting. We were happy for them, but their announcements also filled us with grief as we continued to face the feeling of loss month after month.

Five years into applying for new jobs, I finally got offered a role as an injury prevention health promoter. This was a much less stressful job, and after just six months of being in it, we fell pregnant. After nine years of marriage and sadness we welcomed Pieta, our bundle of joy, into our lives. 'Pieta' means 'sculpture', and she was named after my late father, Peter. Pieta brought with her some much-needed happiness, and almost six years later, after another season of difficulty to conceive, she was followed by a younger brother, Flynn. Flynn completed our family and brought a much-needed sense of life with his fun and high energy.

Becoming a mum and no longer working full time meant a change in focus for me. I became heavily involved with establishing a non-profit community group with some friends, running self-esteem courses for women and children. We also moved to a new church where we took on leadership positions, and Lincoln returned to work full time. These were all huge steps forward for our family; however, the ups and downs of Lincoln's condition were a reality we lived with—and still live with. At any moment, his back can flare up and he can be immobile for several days or weeks, leaving me to carry the load. In the back of our minds there is always the worry of whether the torn disc will rupture, or whether discs further up, which now carry extra stress after an additional fusion, will do the same.

Once the intensity of the years immediately following Lincoln's accident and our infertility journey were over, we enjoyed a more settled season of life without any serious challenges for some time. But in the year leading up to going to ministry school, life felt heavy again. We were experiencing significant stresses, as were many people who we loved, and we found ourselves supporting family and friends through death, sickness, and marriage breakups, all while navigating a change in the leadership of the non-profit organization that required me to take on more responsibility—all during a once-in-a-lifetime pandemic which no one had any experience in!

After the death of a close friend's teenage son, I wrestled with God, asking why so often we don't see healings and miracles in our lives. They were in the Bible; I had faith for them, yet I hadn't seen any happen, even though we had contended consistently for Lincoln's healing. This wrestle led me to enrol in an online 'School of Faith' that taught about healings and miracles.

One night, during the online class, I was feeling weighed down by the responsibility of leadership when I had an incredible God-encounter. I saw Jesus walk up to me, and He whispered in my ear, "The joy of the Lord is your strength." Tickling my side, He spun me around and danced me around the room like a dad would to his little girl. He then flicked me up onto His shoulders so that I could see high above the scenery and out in the distance. As we looked out together, He told me that He would carry me through this season of greater responsibility and that His joy would be my strength. I could feel His strong arms around my legs and I knew I was fully supported.

In the days and weeks that followed, I felt lighter, and the burden of leadership seemed like it was gone. Whenever I felt the heaviness start to creep back, I would imagine myself sitting on Jesus' shoulders, looking above the problems. I see now that I'd been given a glimpse of the power of the joy of the Lord; the seed had been planted in me to hunger for more joy.

MORE THAN A CHOICE

How I wish someone had taught me about supernatural joy early on in my life. Growing up in the church, joy wasn't really taught about, and when it was, the message was about making a decision in times of trial to rejoice in the Lord. For years I had focused on 'choosing joy', on having a positive attitude and considering my words carefully knowing that "death and life are in the power of the tongue" (Proverbs 18:21 ESV). I had learnt to 'count my blessings' and would spend time with the Holy Spirit, giving Him my burdens—but while it helped, I still seemed to have only just enough joy to get by.

What I was witnessing at ministry school was different. It wasn't 'just enough', and it didn't fluctuate according to people's feelings or circumstances; it was something they carried. It wasn't from their natural man; it was supernatural. Their example, along with my experience of overflowing joy 'running down my leg', drove me to start looking for a book to teach me more about this supernatural joy. I'm a thinker and an avid reader, so I wanted to understand joy more from a biblical, intellectual, and Spirit-filled perspective. I wanted to know how to get it, how to maintain it, and how to give it away like my teacher. I hunted high and low for such a book, but I couldn't find what I was looking for anywhere.

So, I started reading anything I could find, voraciously searching for online articles by Christian writers. I didn't quite get what I was expecting. I may have only had a taste of 'supernatural joy', but I knew that what I was reading wasn't giving me the full picture—at times it even sucked the joy out of me, leaving me with more questions. According to some of these writers, joy was nothing more than 'the ability to be content believing that God is working all things for our good', or 'steadiness; the settled assurance that God is in control of all the details of my life and the quiet confidence that ultimately, everything is going to be alright'. One article described joy as 'maturity wrought from experience, with a little heartache and faith mixed in; the determined choice to praise God in every situation and to respond to external circumstances with inner contentment and satisfaction because we know that God will use these things to accomplish His Word in and through our lives'. One magazine article for busy moms even suggested that we could experience relief from the weight of our responsibilities and the tediousness of the tasks of our day by finding a 'moment' of joy in reading some scriptures on the topic. *A moment? Is that all I could hope for?*

So many emotions and thoughts went through my mind as I continued to research, but mostly it was disbelief. *Joy is contentment? Maturity with faith and heartache mixed in? A determined choice?* I had done that for years, yet I wasn't overflowing with joy. And while some writers referenced the 'extreme happiness with which the believer contemplates salvation and the bliss of the afterlife', no one gave a reason for having joy *now*. Contemplating another forty years of life before I get to heaven to find joy sounded depressing to me. *Didn't Jesus promise an abundant life, not an abundant afterlife?* I just couldn't get over how these Christian writers had so little hope or expectation of joy in their lives, yet they were the ones writing on the subject! *Why was our expectation for joy so low?*

I started to ask the Holy Spirit about this. I knew that Satan is called a thief who comes to steal, kill, and destroy (John 10:10). *Had he lied to us about joy?* Had he destroyed our understanding of joy, making us content with peace and hope, or trying to find it in our own strength? Had he stolen our expectation of how much joy is truly available in the Christian life?

I wondered if he had waged war on our joy because he knows that the joy of the Lord is our strength (Nehemiah 8:10). Was there a strength to be found that he didn't want us to access? I contemplated my experiences of joy and how attractive it is—how the example of joy-filled Christians made me hungry for more. Was the enemy purposely trying to steal our joy because he knows how effective and compelling it is, and what a powerful evangelistic tool it is? Imagine churches full of joyful people who have strength despite their burdens and are crowned with a beauty that makes others think *I want that too!*

I began studying every verse that I could find about joy, and as I did, I found myself being transformed as my understanding and beliefs about what has been promised to us began to change (Romans 12:2).

REGAINING OUR EXPECTATION FOR JOY

Proverbs 10:28 says, "the hope of the righteous is joy" (CSB). Worldly hope refers to a wish, or a mere desire for something good to happen, but biblical hope is different. Biblical hope is a confident expectation. It has a moral certainty to it. If we were to go one step further and substitute the Hebrew word used for hope in this verse, *tohelet*, with the Greek alternative found in the New Testament, the meaning would shift from 'the expectation of the righteous is joy', to, 'the *guarantee* of the righteous is joy, through Jesus'.

As I meditated on some of the Scriptures in Isaiah about joy, I noticed the repetition of the word 'shall' (Isaiah 35:10; 51:11; 61). This indicates that joy is associated with a promise, command or determination; there's a certainty to it. The passages in Isaiah tell us that five things "shall" happen:

the ransomed shall return to Zion; everlasting joy shall be upon their heads; they shall obtain, or be overtaken with, joy and gladness; sorrow and sighing shall flee; and, there shall be singing and praise.

Early on in the Bible, the word 'Zion' is used to refer to a physical place, a hill where the most ancient areas of Jerusalem stood, or the city of Jerusalem itself. Later on, however, it refers to the dwelling place of God both presently in our hearts, and for eternity in heaven. Jesus quoted Isaiah 61:1-3 in Luke 4, thereby asserting that He was anointed by the Spirit to bestow everlasting joy to us, the ones that He had come to redeem.

Sadly, many people miss out on these promises because they think that Zion is only referring to heaven, rather than being here on earth, within us; that this everlasting joy is only available in eternity, rather than being available for us now. But the Apostle Paul teaches that the Kingdom of God is righteousness, peace, and joy in the Holy Spirit (Romans 14:17), and Jesus said that the Kingdom is within us (Luke 17:21). So joy cannot just be for our eternal future! Why would we need joy in heaven anyway? Doesn't Revelation say that there will be no more death, mourning, crying or pain, and that in heaven, God will wipe every tear from us (Revelation 21:4)? God, the source of joy, is going to be there with us! Isn't it here on earth that we could use more joy?

When we reflect on what is promised in these verses, it is mind-blowing. Everlasting joy on our heads *now*, being overtaken with joy and gladness *now*, sighing and sorrow flee *now*, as we come to Zion, God's presence, with singing! Can you imagine what this would look and feel like if we actually took hold of it? This is the joy we should be expecting in our lives—not just when we get to heaven.

One day as I was journaling, the Holy Spirit said to me,

"Kyllie, more is available in me—more joy, more peace, more grace. Joy is an untapped resource by many Christians. They need to know that much more is

available. It's not what they do, it's what I do. I crown you; I pour out joy on you; I wash you; I anoint your head; I fill you. My joy protects you, strengthens you, and sustains you. My joy heals and releases those who are held captive. You need to challenge the lies. You need to start with the church, and then it will overflow to the community. It will change generations."

Let's stop imagining what it would look like to live with joy, and instead step into it. Let's challenge the lies and bring the change that not only the church is longing for, but the world.

ACTIVATION

Sit with the Lord and talk to Him about your beliefs around joy. Be willing to have your current thinking challenged and to repent of any lies you have been believing, as you invite Him to renew your mind with the truth of what His Word says about joy. Trust that the Holy Spirit wants to and will be faithful to "guide you into all truth" (John 16:13) as you open your heart to learn. As you have these conversations with God, you may find it helpful to journal, asking Him a question and then writing down His response. You may also find it helpful to ponder some of the following questions as you process your understanding of joy with God:

1. How have you defined joy in your life? Have you seen it as something to choose? As simply counting your blessings?

2. Do you believe joy is for now, or something that awaits us in eternity? Read Romans 14:17 and Luke 17:21. Why is joy a hallmark of the Kingdom, and what does it mean to you that the Kingdom is within you?

3. As you have read this chapter how has your understanding of joy changed? What revelations have you had about your beliefs on joy?

4. Describe your level of expectation for joy in your life.

CHAPTER THREE

The Person of Joy

In Your presence is fullness of joy.
Psalm 16:11 NASB

It is often said that great difficulties will either draw you closer to God or drive you further away from Him. I'm grateful to be able to say that for me, the former has been true. Years of strife and stress, coupled with a sense of desperation, drew me closer to the Lord than I had ever been before. When it felt like no one else understood what I was going through, He was my safe space to process, the One who I could rely on. Because of this, I am now grateful for those years and have reached the point where, despite how incredibly hard they were, I wouldn't wish them away even if I could (although I would want my husband to have been spared crippling pain). Without them, I don't think we would have learnt the lessons we did or have the depth of faith in Christ that we now enjoy.

Hardship led me to cling to God, which I loved; however, the intimacy forged through hardship presented a surprising challenge for me: I found that once the struggles began to subside and our life started to settle into a more 'normal' rhythm, so too did the need and the want for God. I remember coming to a point where I recognized I didn't know how to have a close relationship with God when my life was going well. At times, part of me even longed for some sort of difficulty to come along so I could be closer to the Lord again. I know, it sounds ridiculous. *Why would I want life to be harder? Why would I want difficulty to return after years of pleading for God to take it away?* The answer is: Because I hungered for intimacy with the Lord more than anything else. I needed to learn to do my relationship with the Lord differently, and not rely on crises to maintain my connection with Him.

SHIFTING THE FOCUS

When I enrolled in ministry school, I was hungry for more of God. I still am. I had experienced His salvation, His love, His forgiveness and comfort, but I wanted to experience more of His power. I wanted to learn about signs and wonders and healings and miracles. And so, I arrived at Bethel eager to learn the principles of healing. But what I discovered is that the 'more' and the miraculous are not about principles or tools; they are about the Prince and His presence. I've had to shift my focus away from the things I can do, in order to become more aware of God and how He is guiding me.

I began to ponder the need to seek God's face (as in, His presence), not His hands and feet (His blessings). This raised questions in my mind. Was it right to be seeking God for more joy in my life? In doing so, was I prioritizing His 'hands and feet' over His face? I mulled over this question time and again and finally reached this conclusion: Yes *and* no.

Let me explain. The Bible tells us that we can approach God and ask *anything* according to His will (1 John 5:14). It also tells us that if we ask, it will be given; if we seek, we will find; and if we knock, the door will be opened (Matthew 7:7). If the joy of the Lord is a promise, we can be confident that it is the Father's will to give it to us—so why wouldn't He want us to come to Him and ask for it?!

On the other hand, God is likened to a parent. If our children were stressed or hurting, we would want them to seek us out and ask for help. We would be saddened if they felt they couldn't simply come and ask. But if our children only ever came to see us when they wanted or needed something, the relationship would be unsatisfying. In the same way, God wants more in the relationship than just being the 'giver of good gifts'.

The truth is, God has a greater capacity for relationship and for generosity than we can imagine! We see this illustrated in the parable of the prodigal son. The word 'prodigal' means, 'spending money or resources freely and recklessly; wastefully extravagant; having or giving something on a lavish scale'. When we understand this, we see that Luke 15 is not just a story about a prodigal son, it's also about a prodigal father.

In case you're not familiar with this parable, let me recap it quickly for you: The youngest son of the family comes to his father and asks for his inheritance early. Because this was not typically given until after the father's death, in doing so, he was essentially saying to his father, "I wish you were dead." Despite this insult, the father graciously gives his son what he has asked for. The son then recklessly wastes his inheritance on partying. With his money gone and the land in severe famine, he finds himself looking after pigs in order to make ends meet—the worst possible job for a Jewish boy, as pigs were considered 'unclean'. The Bible tells us that when he realizes that even the servants in his father's house are better off than him, he comes to his senses and sets off home to ask his father for forgiveness and a place amongst the servants.

The father's response is completely undignified and extravagant. From a distance, he sees his son returning home, and, filled with compassion, he closes the gap between them by running to him. There is no condemnation—only a warm embrace sealed with a kiss.

But the father doesn't stop there. When the son begins his planned repentance speech, telling him, "I am no longer worthy to be called your son" (v.21), his father cuts him off before he can even ask to work for him, instructing his servants:

> *"Quick! Bring the best robe and put it on him. Put a ring on his finger and sandals on his feet. Bring the fattened calf and kill it. Let's have a feast and celebrate. For this son of mine was dead and is alive again; he was lost and is found."*
> Luke 15:22-24

The son had spent his money recklessly, but the father also gave on a lavish scale. In placing a ring on his son's finger, he affirms his sonship and testifies to his rightful position in his father's household; he was giving his child back his identity.

The story of the prodigal son is a beautiful one, but sadly our familiarity with it often causes us to miss the depth of its message and the extent of our Father in heaven's extravagance towards us. Yes, it may wound God's father-heart if we only come to Him when we want something, but He has an infinite capacity to love us *and* to be generous to us. He welcomes us in whatever condition we come; He wants us to know what it is to be His beloved children. Like the prodigal father, He waits patiently for us to come to Him. And when we do, we get more than we have asked for, because He, too, is reckless in His giving.

This is what it is like when we ask for something we know is in His will, such as more joy. He gives us what we are seeking, but we get more than what we bargained for. We come seeking *something* but instead we get *someone*. The prodigal son was merely looking for a roof over his head and food in his stomach; instead, his relationship with his father was restored, and as a result, he received all the benefits that flowed out of that relationship. Yes, seeking God only for what He can give us, and treating Him much like a wishing well or magic wand, can be a sign of an immature faith, but as Bill Johnson wisely said, "When you find the hand of God, it doesn't take much to then find His face. All you need to do is look up."

This is not said to encourage you to settle for an immature faith but to remind you that we are all flawed humans who need to start somewhere.

THE PERSON OF JOY

We are each on a journey, and God is willing to work with what we can, or are willing to, offer at the time.

I imagine that once he was reunited with his father, the prodigal son soon realized that their relationship was worth more than what he could get from him, even appreciating the many blessings that came with being a son. This is true for our heavenly Father also. Matthew 6:33 tells us that when we seek first the Kingdom of God and His righteousness, all the things we need will be added to us—like the prodigal son, we will experience an overflow of blessing because of whose children we are.

As God has been giving me fresh understanding of stories such as this one, along with encounters God has given me with Him, time and again I have been reminded that joy cannot be reduced to principles, but rather it is about relationship with the joyful One—with the One, or Ones, who *are joy*.

FINDING JOY IN THE TRINITY

Have you ever stopped to consider that joy is available through each member of the Trinity? Often we have a member of the Trinity that we gravitate to, but as I have gone on this journey of seeking joy, I've come to understand that each member of the Trinity has a unique expression of this quality that they invite us to experience. Let me explain . . .

In Zephaniah we read: "The LORD your God is in your midst, a victorious warrior. He will rejoice over you with joy, He will be quiet in His love, He will rejoice over you with shouts of joy" (3:17 NASB). Some versions say "He will joy over you with singing." Imagine that, the God of the universe singing and shouting joy over you! I particularly love the Amplified translation:

> *He will be quiet in His love, [making no mention of your past sins], He will rejoice over you with shouts of joy.*

Sounds like the prodigal father to me—celebrating his son but not mentioning his sins!

Then there is Jesus, who carried "more joy than any of His companions" (Hebrews 1:9), and who said, "These things I have spoken to you so that My joy may be in you, and *that* your joy may be made full" (John 15:11 NASB). He wants us to carry more joy than those around us do! And last, but not least, we read in Galatians 5:22-23 (NASB) that "the fruit of the Spirit is love, *joy*, peace, patience, kindness, goodness, faithfulness, gentleness, and self-control."

So, *the Father* releases joy over us through shouts and singing. *Jesus*, who had more joy than anyone around Him, promises that this same level of joy will be in us, and that it will be complete. And the *Holy Spirit* realizes that promise, by producing the fruit of joy in our lives.

Why then are so many Christians not joyful? I believe it is because we are yet to learn how to access the joy that is available to us.

BEHOLDING AND BECOMING

Psalm 16:11 tells us that in God's presence is fullness of joy, and 2 Corinthians 3:18 shows us that 'what we behold, we become'. Presence, in both the Hebrew and Greek, is a reference to a person's face—to see their face is to be *in their presence*. To 'behold' means 'to fix the eyes upon; to see with attention; to observe with care'. So, if we fix our eyes on God's face or person, will we become what we fixate on? If we behold God's joy will we become more joyful? Absolutely!

Consider Moses, who was up on the mountain with God for forty days. During that time, his singular focus was God. Every day was spent gazing at God's face and His glory, and when he came back down from the mountain, his own face emanated the glory of God (Exodus 34:29). He literally became what he beheld.

This phenomenon of becoming like what we behold was documented in a scientific study where people were asked to judge the looks, personalities, and ages of one hundred and sixty married couples. The participants were given photographs of the men and women as individuals and not told who was married to whom. Researchers found that they consistently judged people who were married as being similar in appearance and personality and that the longer a couple had been together, the more similar they appeared to the participants.[1] If a man will come to look like his bride by staring at her over the years, how much more will the Bride of Christ come to look like Christ by beholding Him?

Prior to studying these scriptures, I had never considered beholding (or, fixing my attention on) the joy of the Lord. I had fixed my attention on His love and perhaps even His peace, but never His joy. So, while I was writing, I thought I would try it. Although God speaks to me through pictures, I am not generally a person who 'sees' in the spirit or in the heavenlies, so I used my imagination to gaze on the joy of each member of the Trinity.

First, I imagined the Father rejoicing over me with singing and shouts of joy. He was too big for me to see fully, but I caught a glimpse of His feet and sandals as He hitched up His robe and began to dance as He sang over me. Caught up in the overflow of His joy, I found myself chuckling. And then it hit me: The reason God was singing and shouting for joy was because of *me;* it was all for *me!* This filled my heart with so much warmth I actually felt overwhelmed, and had to sit with it for quite some time.

Next, I imagined looking at the face of Jesus. I saw Him as a big brother. Grabbing me, He spun me around and danced with me like we were at a celebration. He was the life of the party! I couldn't help but wonder if that was why Jesus was always getting invitations to weddings and dinners, and why kids loved Him so much.

To be honest, I found it harder to fix my gaze on the Holy Spirit. Because He is spirit and doesn't have a form, it was more difficult to visualize Him—

---

1. Personality and Individual Differences, Volume 40 (April 2006) pages 973-984

until I realized that *I* am His form; He is *in me*. As I drew my attention to the Holy Spirit's presence within me, I felt a gentle sensation move through my body and received a 'kiss' on my lips. I felt the joy of being loved.

This is not the only time I have experienced a kiss from heaven. The first was when I was isolating in my room with my second bout of Covid. I had a splitting headache, and hadn't showered or cleaned my teeth in a day and a half because of how intensely my head hurt whenever I moved. I was talking to God about how rotten I felt and my overwhelming sense of isolation, when all of a sudden I became aware of the nearness of the Holy Spirit. My chapped lips felt slightly oily and had a mildly sweet taste I had never experienced before. It was as though an ointment had been placed on my lips. *How did I know that this was the Holy Spirit?* Well, I can tell you that it definitely wasn't me—there was nothing sweet about my mouth or lips that day! Since then, I have experienced that same sensation quite frequently, and each time it is a reminder of how close the Lord is to me and how much He loves me.

I believe that this is the Father's heart for all of His children—that we would know and 'taste' the joy that exists within the Trinity, and that as we learn to behold them, their joy would become our own.

ACTIVATION

I invite you to 'behold' the joy of the Lord. Choose a member (or all) of the Trinity, then read the following verses, noting how each of them minister joy to God's people:

Zephaniah 3:17

Hebrews 1:9

John 15:11

Galatians 5:22-23

Now take some time to gaze upon the joy of each member of the Trinity. What do you see and feel? Journal about your experience.

CHAPTER FOUR

The Position of Joy

*Splendor and majesty are before him; strength
and joy are in his place.*
1 Chronicles 16:27 ESV

I am no poster child for joy—honestly, it's almost comical that I am writing this book. God sure has a sense of humor! As a New Zealander, I come from conservative British stock, and growing up, I was self-conscious and often melancholy. Those who knew me in my younger years would be able to testify that I could be quite introverted at times and rather serious. I had the tendency to plan things well in advance and was most definitely *not* the extroverted, happy-go-lucky, free-spirited child you would expect to end up writing a book about joy. Neither did I come from a charismatic church background where joy was flowing on a regular basis. To be honest, when the Holy Spirit started to take me on this journey of learning about the joy of the Lord, my initial response was, *really God, joy?* I had not traveled halfway across the world to find joy. I had come to Redding to learn, to gain skills, and to increase in my faith for the miraculous—because faith is a serious job, you know. Luckily, the Father knows what we need even when we don't, and He knew that I needed to discover the importance of joy and stop limiting it to a particular personality type, culture, or church denomination. But this wasn't going to be possible without the help of the Holy Spirit.

OUR ADVANTAGE: THE GIFT OF THE HOLY SPIRIT

Although my church upbringing limited my experience of the Holy Spirit to hearing His quiet voice and left me somewhat suspicious of His 'other' activities, I still possessed a curiosity about Him. Later in life, I had the opportunity to visit churches from more charismatic denominations and would always go up for prayer if they offered it. But alongside my curiosity was a resistance—I still wasn't quite sure what I thought about all the laughing and falling over, and I was aware of the unspoken expectation that I *would* fall over when being ministered to. Whenever people put their hands on my head to pray for me, I would lock my knees and dig in my heels. I was determined no one was going to push me over; I only wanted to fall if it was under the weight of God's presence. Over time, however, I became more comfortable with the demonstrable signs of the Holy Spirit's activity. And then, one Sunday in my late twenties when life felt at its bleakest, I experienced His power for myself.

Desperate for breakthrough, I had gone up to the front after a church service, for prayer. As the worship team sang, asking the Holy Spirit to rain down and His power to fall, I stood there quietly singing along with them. The pastor was working his way down the line praying for people and was still several people away from me when, out of nowhere, it was as though my knees were kicked out from under me and I crumpled to the ground. It felt like I was surrounded by light.

Twenty minutes or so later, I got off the floor, slightly shocked and perplexed by the experience, but feeling more peaceful. After the service one of the 'catchers' came up and apologized to me for not catching me—he'd had no idea that I was going to go down, as no one was anywhere near me. The Holy Spirit had ministered to me without any human assistance so that I would know without a doubt that it was Him! I've heard people say that the Holy Spirit is a gentleman. Well, in my experience

He is—until He's not!

That day, my mind was opened to the reality that there is more to the Holy Spirit than just His quiet voice, and ever since, He's been gently teaching and stretching me to hear and experience Him in different ways.

Have you ever stopped to consider how lucky we are to have the Holy Spirit with us? Not just His voice, but also His power and His presence? In the Garden of Eden, Adam and Eve freely walked and talked with the Lord, but after tasting the forbidden fruit, they were cast away from His presence. In an instant, everything changed, not only for them, but for all of humanity as intimate relationship with God was lost. Their ability to speak directly with God was now limited, and the way God communicated with them changed too. Messages were often delivered through an intermediary and tended to be addressed to the people as a whole rather than individually. Over time, God's voice was heard less and less frequently—just think about some of the 'greats' in the Old Testament and how often God communicated with them. He spoke to Noah five times over 950 years, Abraham, who was called God's friend, eight times over 175 years, and then Isaac twice, and his wife, Rebekah, once, over 180 years. There was even a stretch of time where He didn't speak for 400 years!

But one figure in the Old Testament points to how God would restore the intimacy that had been lost: David. David was anointed king, and we're told that from that day on, "the Spirit of the Lord came powerfully upon David" (1 Samuel 16:13). Others had experienced the Holy Spirit's anointing for a moment, or to carry out a specific purpose, but He *remained* on David, giving us a glimpse of what was to come—of what it would look like to carry the very presence of God in our lives and converse freely with Him again.

Then came Jesus, the One who would make this restored relationship possible. The disciples got a taste of what it was like to do life with God dwelling among them, but even they weren't constantly with Jesus while He was on earth. It wasn't physically possible; Jesus could only be in one place at a time. So, as His time drew near to return to heaven, He spoke to them of the Holy Spirit, who would now be the One to teach them and be with them until the end of time. Jesus even went so far as to say, "It is to your advantage that I am leaving; for if I do not leave, the Helper will not come to you" (John 16:7 NASB). Through the indwelling of the Holy Spirit, Jesus would now be able to be with His people *always* and *everywhere*; they would never be alone. Not only that, but the Holy Spirit would enable His joy to be in them—in us—and it would be complete (John 15:11).

Jesus made this promise of joy to His disciples in His last few hours with them. He had just washed their feet, predicted both His betrayal by Judas and His denial by Simon Peter, and prepared them for the fact that He was going away to a place where they could not follow. The disciples were confused, desperate, and grieving. I'm sure joy was not on their radar. And yet, that was what Jesus promised. But He didn't only promise it, He also shared with them the key to joy—abiding in Him.

RETHINKING JOHN 15

One of my classes at Bethel was called "The Amazing Power of In." The teacher was incredibly passionate, and using John 15-17, particularly the image of the vine and the branches, he described the necessity of remaining (or, abiding) in Christ, our position in Christ, and the wonder of what we received from Him when we invited Him into our lives. His teaching dispelled many misconceptions about our connection to Christ and the 'struggle to abide' that I had heard preached. He also addressed the belief that many hold that the Gardener's pruning is harsh—that He will ruthlessly cut you off and throw you into the fire if you are not fruitful enough. This class showed me that these ideas stem from our faulty understanding of what it means to be 'the branches'.

THE POSITION OF JOY

You've likely heard it taught that you are 'grafted' or 'plugged' into the vine; however, neither of these words accurately convey what the image of the vine and the branches truly represent in John 15. They both imply that there is a weakness to the connection and can make us feel like it is easy to become detached from the vine.

Let me ask you: What parts of the grapevine are the vine? *The roots? The trunk? The branches? The leaves? The fruit?* The answer is simple: All of these parts are the vine! This means the branch is not separate from the vine, it *is* the vine.

Now a second question: Where does the branch start and the vine stop? Again, the answer is simple: *It doesn't!* When you look at a grapevine you can't see any separation between the branch and the rest of the vine; the branch is the vine, and the vine is the branch. This is such a beautiful picture of our union with Christ: I am in Him, and He is in me, there is no separation. We are one, and all I need to do is remain, or abide, in this union.

The word 'abide' is repeated some twelve times in the first seventeen verses of John 15, but just as we often fail to understand what it is to be the branch, we also struggle to know what it means to abide in Christ. As we rethink what Jesus was saying to us, it's helpful to compare the English, Hebrew, and Greek words for abide. In English, abide simply means 'to live or dwell'. The Hebrew word used in the Old Testament, *yashab*, encompasses these same ideas, but links the concept of interpersonal relationships to being in a shared space. The word means: 'to haunt, lurk, inhabit, marry; to bring again to a place'. This 'abiding' refers to a deep and personal relationship. It is more than simply resting in one place; it is about maintaining personal connections there. Likewise with the Greek word, *menō*. This includes many of the same concepts as the English and the Hebrew, but also has the added concept of staying—and continuing to stay. It could be viewed as the difference between taking up long-term residency versus staying somewhere temporarily or on vacation.

So when Jesus talks about us abiding in Him and Him in us, He's inviting us to live with Him in a state of cohabitation; to maintain our connection with Him, and to stay in that place of intimacy with Him. But this remaining is not one-sided, nor is it solely reliant on our efforts and actions. Rather, it is about dependency upon the Holy Spirit who dwells within us to maintain our connection.

Once we understand what it means to abide, we will be able to recognize the lie that it is easy to lose our connection with God; that sin and wrong desires will sever us from the vine. Think about it—in life, the hard part is getting up! Have you ever been sitting on the couch when you're tired? You know you should get ready for bed, but you're desperately trying to find the energy and motivation to get up and go! In that moment, you are abiding with the couch. You are remaining on the couch, you are dwelling there—and you're not having to work hard at it!

Let's apply this to the branch: Does the branch have to work to remain in the vine? No. Rather it has to work at being disconnected from the vine. It takes a violent act or a slow 'hacking away' day by day—something the branch would be well aware of—for a branch to be cut off.

Abiding or remaining in Christ is the most natural thing to do. It is not an effort; it is a 'staying' empowered by the gift of the Holy Spirit. He is the One who enables the Father and Son to make their home in us (John 14:23); we simply remain there with them, and when we do, joy abounds. In the words of 1 Chronicles 16:27, "Strength and joy are in his dwelling place." This means strength and joy are in you and me. But as we've seen, Jesus doesn't just want His joy to be in us—He wants it to be complete; He wants us to have the full measure of the joy that is available to us. John 15 teaches us that one of the ways He increases our joy is through pruning.

GREATER JOY

Let's be honest, we like the image of abiding that the vine and the branch illustrates, *but the pruning and the cutting of the vine?* Not so much. In fact, the image has often been a cause of fear for believers. Nobody wants to have to endure pain in order to bear more fruit, and the thought of being cut off (v.2), or worse still, burnt for not remaining in Christ, is terrifying (v.6). But if Scripture tells us that "perfect love drives out fear" (1 John 4:18), then surely God's activity in our lives should not be something we are afraid of?

Our understanding of who God is will shape how we understand what Jesus is teaching us in this passage. If we view God through the lens of a harsh, authoritarian father, we will approach these verses with fear and trembling, feeling like we have to work hard at remaining in order to avoid punishment. But if we believe that He is loving and kind, then we will be able to trust His work in our lives and accept His invitation to rest and abide in Him.

Our God is a compassionate and careful Gardener. He doesn't just cut off a struggling branch. If it is still attached and has signs of life, He will care for it. He will prop it up, support it with string, bandage it, nourish it with good food, and nurse it back to health. His heart is to see all people saved (1 Timothy 2:4), and so He goes to great lengths to tend to His branches. He will only clear a branch away when, after much effort and time with many opportunities to grow and thrive, there is absolutely no change and no sign of life. Like any gardener who maintains their garden, He removes the dead wood. But we need to remember that the branch can only die if it has become disconnected from the source of life. To die will take effort on our part—we will have to remove ourselves fully from Him, either with a violent act or a gradual 'sawing away' over time. Becoming a dead branch is no easy feat, and there is no need to fear it happening by mistake.

Just as there is care in His cutting, there is also care in His pruning. When I think about having to be pruned in order to bear more fruit, I associate this process with difficulty, pain and loss. For most of my childhood the most popular Bible translation was the New King James Version, and it used the word 'purge' rather than prune, which adds a sense of violence and force to what is taking place. The original Greek word that Jesus uses in verse two, however, actually means 'to cleanse' or 'to prune trees and vines from useless shoots.' When we think of pruning in this light, it depicts a gentler, more nurturing, process.

Let me share with you a time when the Holy Spirit cleansed me through cutting off useless shoots, gently trimming away lies I was believing, in order that I would bear greater fruit, greater joy...

It was October 2020, just two months after we had started ministry school, and I found myself physically and emotionally spent. After fighting so hard to get to America only to have arrived and caught Covid and find school was now online, I was wrestling with deep disappointment. Here we were in a new country, with no family, few friends, and having to do school in isolation after spending so much time and energy, and thousands of dollars in the process. I started to question what we were doing here. We could have stayed at home and studied online, which would have taken far less effort and been much less expensive.

That particular day, I remember lying on the couch crying, complaining, and having a good old pity party while the worship was happening in my online class. I let rip with God, expressing all my emotions and letting Him know just how hacked off I was with the situation. I won't write exactly what I said as it might shock you, but you get the idea. I was not happy.

Then the Holy Spirit quietly asked me a question: "If I had told you this was going to happen, would you have come anyway?"

"Of course," I replied. "You have never confirmed something so many times. We knew we had to come."

He gently challenged me, "So what are you complaining about then? Get over yourself."

Just then the worship team started to sing about the crushing and pressing and yielding required to produce new wine. As I lay there and listened to the music, I knew I needed to yield to the Lord and the process He had for me. In that moment of surrender, I realized that I was believing the lie that I was going to miss out—that with the course being online I would miss out on the full experience of everything the school had to offer. The truth is, God knew better. He knew that being online for a period and being isolated would strengthen my relationship with Him. In making it less about the corporate atmosphere and relationships, it became more about intimacy with Him.

I needed that God-conversation that day to cleanse me from the lies I was believing so that I could have joy. But that cleansing or 'pruning' was done in the context of relationship, through communicating and abiding in Jesus. It wasn't a painful experience, but gentle and fruitful. Imagine the fruit that might have grown if I had continued to believe the lie that I wouldn't get what I needed. It could have led to a year of bitterness, of shutting down, grumbling and complaining, or even leaving prematurely. It could have meant that I didn't receive the revelation of supernatural joy that I received over the following six months.

The Father, our good Gardener, knew what would be most beneficial to me, and in the same way that He cared about my fruitfulness—my joy—He cares about yours. You don't have to strive to be more joyful, you simply need to rest and abide in the presence of the One who makes all things grow, and let the Holy Spirit do the heavy lifting. Trust the process He has for you—He won't let you miss out.

ACTIVATION

1. How have you understood the illustration of the vine and the branches? Ask the Holy Spirit to identify any lies you may have believed. Ask Him to show you how you need to yield to the Gardener's process.

2. As you go about your week, I encourage you to practice abiding in Christ by being aware of your connection with Him. Recognize His presence with you and in you. What shifts in your heart and environment as you focus your attention more on remaining in that place of relationship?

CHAPTER FIVE

Joy Overflowing

May the God of hope fill you with all joy . . . so that you may overflow with hope by the power of the Holy Spirit.
Romans 15:13

Not long after my experience of joy 'leaking' down my leg, we met with our revival group (a weekly meeting of sixty students assigned to a pastor), and I shared with them about how the Lord had spoken to me through a spilled cup of coffee and a Sunday School song. As I relayed what had happened and spoke about the joy of the Lord, more joy flowed up and out of me. I laughed and shook, and the more I shared the more I laughed, until I secretly wished I had put on my sports bra that morning and not the pretty flimsy one I had worn instead! From then on it became a standing joke amongst our revival group, and every time I laughed, they would ask if joy was 'leaking down my leg'.

But it wasn't all fun and laughter. In the coming months, our resolve and our adaptability would be frequently tested. The Covid virus spread rapidly throughout Redding, and safety protocols shifted just as rapidly, with class changes often being made at a moment's notice. Sometimes we were divided into smaller groups or had class outside in car parks, and eventually, when the weather worsened and winter approached, large tents were hired to house us all. With church services no longer allowed indoors, they made the most of these, holding nightly worship and prayer services where we all rallied to pray for America and the world. We dubbed the tents, 'revival tents'.

By early January 2021, we had been away for five months and Christmas had highlighted just how much I was missing friends and family. I was deeply homesick and struggling with loneliness as the reality of establishing friendships in a new country set in. Compounding the barriers created by the pandemic was the fact that at forty-four years of age I was old enough to be most of the students' mother. My feelings were constantly up and down—it was like riding a roller coaster. My poor husband didn't know who this emotional woman was; I was usually the 'Steady Eddie', the even-keeled one in the relationship. Something needed to change.

A FRESH ENCOUNTER

I'd been invited to go with one of my classmates to an evening service in the revival tent. When we got there, the atmosphere was thick, even electric, with the tangible presence of the Lord. Everyone was worshiping and rejoicing, but I was struggling. I just wasn't feeling it; I felt so flat. I tried to join in, but after an hour or so, the noise and the busyness became too much.

Making my way out of the tent, I stood outside and began to talk with the Lord about my feelings of loneliness even amongst a large crowd. As I continued to worship and pray on my own, I had a vision. In the vision, a large bucket of gold, oily liquid was being poured out over my head. It trickled down my shoulders and back, eventually covering my entire body. I stood there, taking in the sensation and asking the Lord what it was. He revealed to me that the liquid was the oil of gladness, and it was being poured out on me to replace my sadness. That was when I noticed a fine, oily residue covering my hair and the back of my neck—it was even on the inside of my ears. I went home that night feeling different, and when I woke the next morning the homesickness had lifted. From then on, I had a sense of internal stability and the joy I carried seemed more sustained.

The different encounters I was having with the joy of the Lord got me thinking about what joy actually is. I tried to remember if I had heard any teaching on the subject during my years in church, but all I could recall was a few messages about the fruit of the Spirit and rejoicing during trials. I couldn't remember a sermon specifically on the joy of the Lord ever being preached in all my many years of church going. I realized I didn't even know the context for the often-quoted verse from Nehemiah that says the joy of the Lord is our strength (Nehemiah 8:10).

I'm not exactly sure why joy isn't taught more often in the church. Maybe it's because joy can be messy and noisy and can't always be controlled— besides, if you haven't experienced it for yourself, it can seem really weird and hard to understand. I remember my pastor telling me about a time when she had been hit with holy laughter at a conference. People questioned whether it was from God and told her it couldn't be, since her stomach muscles ached afterwards.

Have you ever noticed that we think it's great if someone is overcome with the peace or love of God in church, and even if they're crying loudly because of this encounter, we accept that, but if someone is extremely happy and laughing exuberantly, we question if it's really God? Some even go so far as to attribute it to the enemy. But why would Satan want us to experience joy? In any case, I wanted to know more; I wanted answers so I could share them with others too, so I began to dig deeper into the Word for myself.

CONTINUALLY FILLED

As I studied the Scriptures, I observed an interesting pattern. Joy was often coupled with other words, like all, full, fullness, complete, abundant, and no bounds. For example, in Psalm 16:11 David writes, "In your presence there is *fullness* of joy" (ESV), and in John 15:11 Jesus says, "My purpose for telling you these things is so that the joy that I experience will *fill* your hearts with *overflowing* gladness!" (TPT). We see in Acts 13:52 that the disciples received this promise and "were continually *filled* with joy and with the Holy Spirit" (NASB). Paul, too, knew such a joy, declaring in 2 Corinthians 7:4, ". . . in all our troubles my joy knows *no bounds*." He would go on to pray for us to know this same joy, saying, "Now may the God of hope *fill* you with *all* joy" (Romans 15:13 NASB).

To be 'full' means to 'contain or hold as much as possible, having no empty space, not lacking or omitting anything, complete'. Consider what happens when you fill a cup. When do you know that it is completely full? When it reaches the brim? No . . . when it starts to overflow! That's when you know that there is no more room; it is completely full. So why is there such an emphasis on *all joy* and the *fullness of joy* in the Bible? What is special about joy that requires this emphasis? I believe it's because not only the quality of our joy matters, but also the *quantity*. Much joy is needed to dispel the fear, depression, anxiety, addiction, self-harm and suicide that is so rampant in our culture, our communities, and even the church. It's time for us to begin to place the same importance on joy as Scripture does.

One day I asked the Lord a question I had been pondering: How much is *all* joy, God? How much is available? His response was, "Depends on the need, depends how much needs to be filled." This got me thinking about Romans 5:20, which says, "Where sin increased, grace increased all the more." *Is it true for joy too, that when grief and sorrow increase, greater levels of joy are also available?* 1 Peter 4:13 does say, "to the degree that you share the sufferings of Christ, keep on rejoicing" (NASB), and 2 Corinthians 8:2 tells us that even in severe trials and extreme poverty, the church at Corinth overflowed with joy, revealing that great joy is possible even in challenging circumstances.

In 2 Kings 4 we see a prophetic picture of just how God keeps filling us up with the oil of gladness, even (and perhaps, especially), in times of lack. In this passage we read of a widow whose husband had been among the company of prophets. Since his passing, she had fallen on hard times and was behind on her bills. With creditors coming to take her two sons away as slaves, she cries out to Elisha, the prophet, for help. Luckily, he has a supernatural solution to enable her to pay off her debts. He instructs her to go to her neighbors, collect as many containers as she can find, then pour out the small amount of oil she possessed until each and every one is filled. Miraculously, the oil kept flowing until all the vessels were filled. With that supernatural provision, her needs were met and her bills paid off.

When life leaves us feeling empty or low on joy, God keeps pouring into us until our need, too, is met. This is not a one-time offer, but something that can happen whenever there is lack. Like the disciples in Acts 13, we too can experience a continual filling of joy!

DEFINING JOY

So, what does the *fullness of joy*—overflowing, abundant joy—look like? You would think there would be an easy answer. But when we study the word 'joy' (or its verb form, 'to rejoice') we find that it is used around four hundred times in the Bible, and that amongst those four hundred uses are thirty-five different Hebrew and Greek words, each with a different meaning. Perhaps this is the reason why we struggle to get a clear definition or understanding of biblical joy—there are a myriad of ways that it can be expressed!

Joy is something that we carry; it is 'a glad countenance, a calm delight, a merry heart'. But it is also something that we express; it is 'cheerfulness' and 'exceeding gladness'. And sometimes, it is physically demonstrated—it is to 'leap or jump; to spin around under the influence of a violent emotion'. It can also be audible. Joy can mean 'to shout or cry, to sing triumphantly, to exult and express praise through loud noise and musical instruments'. But some forms of the word joy are not what we expect. Joy can be 'a ringing cry, a shrill sound, or a tremulous sound like a pole shaking in the wind'. If I had to sum it all up and define what I think joy is (it's about time, since we are already at the end of the fifth chapter, right?!), I'd say it's a *feeling of inner gladness or delight,* and that rejoicing is *the act of outwardly expressing our inner joy.*

Interestingly, the word 'laughter' does not appear in any of the biblical definitions but is included in the words *ālaz* and *allîz,* which mean 'the sound of joy', or 'vibration of the voice'. Ironically though, laughter was exactly what came out of my mouth as I studied all these different words. I could envisage them *all* because at some point in the past two years at ministry school I had witnessed or experienced for myself every single one in some shape or form. In my first year of school I laughed, cried, shook, danced, sang, shouted for joy, and praised God loudly. Over my second year, my joy was quieter. I had moments of laughter, but mostly I felt peaceful, calm, and content—perhaps this is best described as a countenance of joy. My introverted side has found it reassuring to see that the quieter expressions of joy are used more frequently in the Bible than the louder ones, yet they still qualify as joy. There's no one 'right' way to be joyful.

I think at times the enemy lies to us hoping to disqualify us. He knows the strength of joy and the power it holds, so he wants to make us believe the lie that we don't carry real joy. If we are carriers of quieter joy, or *chara*, he might tell us that we are not passionate or expressive enough. If we are on the opposite end of the spectrum, he may cause others to question whether the joy we have experienced is biblical, or from God.

At times when I have shared that I am writing a book on this topic, I have gotten perplexed looks and even raised eyebrows. These responses started to make me feel insecure, and I began to doubt whether I should be the one writing on joy, as my outward display of joy had quietened and was no longer measuring up to what myself and others had come to expect. I now realize that I was carrying the gladness of *śāmaḥ* and *chara*-type joy for this season, rather than the loud, exuberant *rānan* or *gîl*-type joy that I had initially experienced.

The joy that we carry makes an impact; it affects the atmosphere of a room and the individuals in it. This was highlighted to me recently when I was serving on a ministry trip. Early in the trip we had formed a prayer line to minister to the leaders of the church. As they walked past us, we would each pray for them. I was second in the line and started to notice a shift in my spirit as different people stepped into the line. An older lady moved towards me and instantly I felt intense peace. As she approached me, I told her, "You carry immense peace," to which she replied, "Yes, shalom peace." I later realized that she was one of the lead pastors who I hadn't yet met. As I continued to pray for other leaders, I encountered five other women and two men who carried that same intensity of peace with them. For a long time I have been told that I carry an atmosphere of peace, but until that point, I had never experienced it in or on others like that. Although this incident was related to peace and not joy, it made me realize how much the overflow of our countenance affects the world around us, even when we aren't always aware of it.

It is so important for us to know what and who we carry, because the world needs it. It needs us to be people who release the full measure of joy that Jesus intended us to, so that they can experience its strength for themselves. Like the people I prayed for, we can become carriers of joy in a real and tangible way. All we need to do is abide and ask. What He did for the widow in 2 Kings 4, He will do for us—He will keep filling us up!

ACTIVATION

Spend some time reviewing the different manifestations of joy in this chapter and consider the following:

1. How would you currently describe your own level of joy in view of all the ways you now know it can be evidenced?

2. Which of these expressions of joy have you personally experienced? Thank the Lord for them.

3. Are there any other types of joy you would like to experience? Ask the Lord to give them to you. Whether His answer comes immediately or in the future (as it did for me), keep asking expectantly.

4. Has the enemy tried to disqualify you in any way with respect to joy? Invite the Holy Spirit to uncover any lies you have been believing, and replace them with truth.

CHAPTER SIX

Joy and Trust

May the God of hope fill you with all joy . . . as you trust in him.
Romans 15:13

Before leaving New Zealand our kids had always lived in the same house, gone to the same school and had the same group of friends, so naturally their well-being was our biggest concern as we got ready for this new adventure. How would they manage such a huge move and the complete upending of their worlds? Would they thrive, or merely survive?

Initially, everything went well. With so many new experiences to be had, they were kept busy, and there was a level of excitement for them about it all. But once we settled into the reality of our new life in America, our ten-year-old daughter began to struggle. As the school year kicked into gear, it quickly became apparent that she was at least two years behind in math. Back home, she had always met or exceeded the required standard, but in her new environment, this wasn't the case. The situation was made more difficult as her math teacher was away for a few weeks and the substitute teacher, who did not know her situation, expected Pieta to complete her homework. Every day for two weeks Pieta came home stressed-out and unable to do her assignments. She would cry and plead with us to take her home; she didn't want to be here anymore. The constant anxiety and bedtime tears took a toll on our family. It was so hard to see our daughter in such distress. We started to worry that we had done the wrong thing, and second guessed our decisions.

Desperate to help my daughter, I took this situation to the Lord, asking Him to show us what to do. As I prayed, God gave me a picture of Pieta sitting outside at a picnic table with her head back and mouth open wide as she laughed out loud. The sun was streaming over her, reflecting off her golden blond hair, her skin was clear, and she looked extremely happy. This beautiful picture comforted my worried mommy-heart. Then within my spirit I heard the Lord say, "She will thrive in this environment." Warm tears filled my eyes and streamed down my face. Pieta was going to be okay! She was going to do better than just survive; she was going to thrive. I could trust that God would take care of her as we kept obediently following His leading.

THE IMPORTANCE OF TRUST

Trust may not be something you have considered in relation to joy. I know I hadn't—in fact, originally this chapter was not even in my book. However, over the course of this journey, I have come to realize just how vital trust is to joy and how interconnected they are. If we are worried, anxious and full of fear, it is almost impossible to be joyful. Paul demonstrates the cause-and-effect relationship between joy and trust for us when he says, "May the God of hope fill you with all joy and peace as you trust in him" (Romans 15:13). In other words, in order to be filled with *all joy* we must first trust in Him.

Many of us will be familiar with this verse:

> *Trust in the Lord with all your heart, and do not lean on your own understanding. In all your ways acknowledge Him, and He will make your paths straight.*
> *Proverbs 3:5-6 NASB*

A verse like this is easy to understand—we *know* we should trust God—but it is much more difficult to put into practice. While some seem to possess faith that never wavers, many of us struggle to remain steadfast, especially in the longer term. We give up in the face of delay, attaching strings to our willingness to trust God, and oftentimes, it can seem easier to take matters into our own hands. But if we want to be filled with *all joy*, we must learn to trust in God rather than our own understanding. So how do we do this?

If we look again at the story of the widow in 2 Kings 4, we see a number of keys relating to trust. Although the story is not directly about trusting God, the confidence that the widow places in Elisha, the man of God, has much to teach us about cultivating a life of faith. As we've already seen, her situation appeared hopeless. With her sons about to be sold into slavery to pay off her debt, she was not only faced with losing her children, but her entire future financial security was at stake. With no social security to fall back on, it was her sons' responsibility to provide for her in her old age. In desperation, she cried out to Elisha for help. This is the first key: *We must turn to God for help.*

So often when we have difficulties in our lives, we try to sort it out ourselves, talking to anyone who will listen. We can tend to come before God more as an afterthought, something we do when we still haven't been able to figure a problem out. We don't have enough of the widow's story to be sure about exactly *when* she decided to go to Elisha for help—maybe she cried out straight away, or perhaps the problem had gone on for some time, long enough for the creditors to be at her door—but what we can see is that she knew *who* to go to. The Bible doesn't say that she went to the neighbors, or even a close friend, but to the man of God. Who do you go to when you are stressed and need solutions to your problems? When you need hope, peace, and joy? We need to trust in the Lord and go to Him *first*.

Secondly, *we must do what He says.*

Elisha responded to the widow by asking her, "How can I help you? Tell me, what do you have in your house?" (2 Kings 4:2). The widow didn't think she had much, but she let him know that she had a small jar of olive oil. That's when Elisha instructed her to find as many jars as she could and to pour her oil into them. Although Elisha's instructions seemed absurd, the widow didn't question or argue with him—she simply followed his directions and did what he asked her to do. Likewise, we may already have the solutions to our problems in our storehouse. We just need the Lord's guidance or courage to be obedient and do what He has said.

When I am faced with obstacles, I love having conversations with God. I've come to look forward to His instructions. The difficulty comes when His answer is not what I expected or the command is not something I want to do. I think that often the hardest directive the Lord gives is to wait. We can be so impatient, especially in our fast-food, high-speed internet, fast turn-around society—and the temptation to take things into our own hands, especially when we are waiting, is great. It's even greater when we have a fixed view of how things should turn out.

How do you respond when the Lord guides you? Do you listen to His direction and submit to His plans? Or do you question and debate, perhaps even choose to do something else? When we trust in the Lord, taking the struggle to Him and choosing to be obedient, He can fill us with peace, hope, and joy in the waiting.

The third key that we find in the widow's story is that *we must not listen to negative voices.*

When I read Bible stories, I like to ask questions about what's not written. Sometimes we don't get as much context as we might in other genres. For example, if we were reading a thriller or a romance novel, we'd find out about the character's emotions and hear their internal dialogue. But we don't often get this in Scripture, so it's left somewhat to our imaginations.

I wonder what the widow was thinking and feeling as she went to the neighbors asking for jars? Did she fear rejection and ridicule? Was she worried about not getting enough jars? After all, Elisha had been specific about not getting too few. Maybe she was demoralized that she had to beg for help. Or perhaps fear for her sons' safety overrode any concern for her own image and reputation.

Then there's the neighbors. I'm sure they would have been well aware of her circumstances and must have thought her request strange, given she had nothing to fill the jars with. Who knows if they questioned her to her face, discouraged her with thoughtless words, or looked down their noses at her, mumbling under their breath how low she had fallen? Regardless, she pressed on with her task. It's so important when we are contending for our circumstances that we don't listen to any fear-based internal dialogue or the negative opinions of others, but instead learn to block out the lies we are hearing, and tune into the truth of what God is saying.

When we were preparing to move to America we had many people question our choices and the likelihood of us being successful in getting there. Some even suggested that we delay going. If we had not listened to God we may have missed out on seeing Him come through for us, on seeing His hand on our circumstances, and on walking in His divine timing. Who knows if I would have gotten to experience God's supernatural joy or even have written this book? It's so important to listen to the guidance the Lord has given you—even if it's just 'wait'—and then to keep reminding yourself of what He has said as you obediently follow through.

The fourth key in the widow's story is that we must *believe God can do the impossible*.

I think the widow must have had some measure of faith to start pouring that day, but I don't imagine it was much. I wonder if she thought, *I'm just pouring oil from one jar to the next. Nothing's going to change except that now my jar will be empty.* She must have been so surprised as the oil continued to flow after that first jar was filled. Perhaps her heart skipped a beat; maybe she began to hold her breath, her expectation growing as one filled jar became two, then three. I have no doubt that with each subsequent jar, her faith would have increased, and her confidence that maybe this was going to work, would have risen.

This is what has happened in my own journey of faith with the Lord. As I have experienced God come through again and again, whether in our finances, prayers for healing, even in things that appear to be coincidences, my faith for the humanly impossible has kept increasing.

Matthew 19:26 says, "With man this is impossible, but with God all things are possible." In your current circumstances, do you believe this verse to be true? When we were planning to come to Bethel, others looked at our situation and called it impossible. They saw the shut embassy, the closed borders and reduced international flights and thought there was no way we would be able to get from New Zealand to America. But due to our history with God and His record of coming through for us in ways we could never have imagined, we knew the words of Matthew 19:26 were utterly trustworthy, that with God all things are possible.

If this hasn't been your experience or you have limited history with God, I want to encourage you to borrow the history—the testimonies—of those around you, and of the heroes of faith recorded for us in Scripture. Allow others' stories to increase your trust and faith that God will come through for you too, in supernatural, miraculous ways.

Finally, *we build trust by knowing Him and being known by Him.* There's a beautiful word in the Hebrew language, and I believe this is the most powerful and critical key when it comes to trust: *yāda'*. Simply put, *yāda'* means 'to know God and be known by Him'. It is to become familiar with His character, His faithfulness, His voice and His presence—to make space for Him to express His heart to us. Likewise, we can share our own thoughts, concerns, fears, desires and dreams with Him. It's not that He doesn't know them already, but that's the essence of relationship—sharing ourselves with another. It is in this place of 'knowing' that He can identity lies we are believing, remind us of the truth, speak into our identity, encourage us, share His love for us, and comfort us through His words and presence. What a gift!

The practical outworking of this principle is seen in Proverbs 3:6 where the instruction to 'acknowledge' the Lord in all our ways is actually to 'yada' Him. Various translations render this verse in a multitude of ways, including 'submit, seek his will, be mindful of, think about him, think on him, remember him, recognize him, acquaint thyself, know him, let him lead you'—so many English words to describe one Hebrew word! The Amplified version beautifully brings together many of these connotations saying: "In all your ways know *and* acknowledge *and* recognize Him and He will make your paths straight and smooth."

When we take all these aspects of *yāda'* and apply them to our lives, we can better understand what it truly means to trust God. For example, if I'm trying to make a decision about something, I can seek out my husband's opinion, acknowledge it, and even be mindful of it, but that's quite different from submitting to his wishes and letting him lead in the situation! *Yāda'* requires and compels me to do *all* of these things because I know the One whom I am trusting to make my paths straight.

Perhaps this is why, before instructing us to 'yada' the Lord in all our ways, we are exhorted to trust in Him with all our heart instead of leaning on our own understanding. It's about heart connection and relationship rather than intellectual knowledge. We can know a person in an intellectual or conceptual way, and even have some personal interactions with them, but this doesn't necessarily mean that we really *know* them. True knowing requires a face-to-face encounter; it takes building history and connection.

The deepest level of *yāda'* is likened to the sexual relationship between a husband and wife, the kind of intimacy where nothing is hidden or held back. Sadly, many Christians know *of* God—they have an intellectual or conceptual understanding of Him—but it doesn't go any further than that. They are missing the intimacy they were intended for.

The widow in 2 Kings had personal experience with Elisha. He was likely a friend of her husband, and she would have heard the stories of how God had moved miraculously through his life. He had parted the sea, purified a town's water source, and prayed and prophesied a victory over the Moabites. She didn't just know *of* him; she *knew* him, had personal experience with him, and more than likely had had face-to-face encounters with him in the past. Having 'yada-ed' him in the past enabled her to trust him with her future.

It's the same for us. When we have experienced the Lord's tangible presence, when we've had a face-to-face encounter and *know* Him, we will find we can trust Him implicitly. For this reason, the key to a greater ability to trust God is to get to know Him in a deeper way, to 'yada' Him! Meditate on Scriptures about His love and faithfulness; feast on testimonies of provision and miracles in whatever area you need breakthrough. Invite others to share their stories. Sit with the Lord and ask Him to show Himself to you. If you struggle to hear God's voice or sense the Holy Spirit, ask others to pray for you, or invite God to reveal Himself to you in your dreams. Do a course on intimacy with God or becoming God's friend. The options are many, but remember, those who diligently seek Him *will* be rewarded (Hebrews 11:6).

LIVING SACRIFICES

My husband's back condition has been the greatest ongoing struggle in my adult life. With my background of physical therapy, I have far too much knowledge about the long-term consequences of spinal fusions;

although they provide stability and relief at the time, in the long run, it puts further stress and strain on the discs and joints above. I am well aware that the disc above Lincoln's two fusions, one of which is already torn, could rupture at any time. This has weighed heavily and frequently on my mind. Lincoln's long-term health and mobility and his healing has been the thing that I have had to give over to the Lord time and again.

During our first two years at Bethel, Lincoln's back was incredibly stable and kept improving. He received a prophetic word about him walking out his healing, and this appeared to be what was happening. In our first year there, he was able to come off all his regular pain relief and nerve medication, despite all the sitting he was doing in class.

Then near the end of our second year of study, Lincoln's back suddenly flared up, and not in its usual spot where he had had previous surgery, but above that level. My mind went into overdrive with all the possibilities of what might happen. I tried to remain calm and supportive for him, but I could tell that he was worried too. One particular day, I left him resting at home watching school online, while I went into classes. I was lonely going without him, and my medical understanding of what was happening in his body was weighing me down.

That day we happened to be discussing a question posed by A.W. Tozer in his book, "The Pursuit of God". The context was the story of Abraham and Isaac. The question Tozer was asking was essentially this: *What were we holding onto that we needed to put on the altar?* Lincoln and I had been discussing his healing, or lack of, and how he had been struggling to give this over to the Lord. I was also wrestling with questions, wondering how we could have the healing ministry that had been prophesied over us without Lincoln's own healing.

During our daily worship time we had been singing a song about being a living sacrifice. As I was singing that day, I saw us putting 'living without Lincoln's healing' onto the altar. I felt the Holy Spirit say, "That's what it means to be a living sacrifice—daily offering up what you hold most precious, most important, most needed, and giving it over to me."

As we continued to worship, I felt prompted to journal. This is a glimpse into what the Holy Spirit impressed upon me:

When we haven't seen healing yet, we live with the daily choice to put it on the altar, to submit to God's plan, to His understanding and not our own. Our sacrifice is being willing to give over our need to understand, and to choose to trust in God and what He is, or seemingly isn't, doing.

I have to give over my need to understand. Why hasn't Lincoln been healed yet, and how can we have a healing ministry if he isn't? Wouldn't it be better to have a testimony of healing? And why would people even want us to pray for them if we haven't yet got victory ourselves?

I have to give over my human understanding and expectations realizing that God has different ways. This is what it means to live as a living sacrifice, placing our questions, our wants, our thoughts, our ideas, our need to know, our right to know, on the altar—giving them over to You, trusting that You have our best interests at heart. In exchange, we receive mercies new every morning, peace that transcends all understanding, and joy that abounds. It's not a one-time thing. It's a daily sacrifice, a daily choice. That's what it means to live as a sacrifice.

As I submitted my fears to the Lord in an act of worship, the Holy Spirit filled me with peace and the knowledge that it would be okay. With hope reignited, I had the inner strength to encourage my husband and continue to pray for his healing. Thankfully, within a week, Lincoln's back settled back down again.

THE REAL MIRACLE

When we think about the miracle in 2 Kings 4, we tend to focus on the jars that overflowed with oil. But I think the real miracle was the turning of sorrow and despair to joy. A hopeless situation was transformed through

JOY AND TRUST

trust and obedience. This is my testimony too.

As I sought the Lord's guidance about my daughter's situation, He showed me the truth and rewarded me with a vision of peace and joy. As I surrendered my greatest fears about my husband's healing, He caused me to abound in hope, and joy returned.

Trust is not about trying harder, being a better Christian, or blindly giving up your will. It's about trusting God with your heart and submitting to Him because of your relationship with Him—because you know Him and are known by Him. This kind of trust makes room for us to be filled with peace, hope, and ultimately, *all* joy!

ACTIVATION

1. Is there anything you are struggling to trust the Lord with? Sit with Him and talk to Him about it. Allow yourself to be *known* by Him.

2. Consider the keys to trusting God. Which key or keys might you need to intentionally activate in this season?

3. Ask the Lord to reveal Himself to you and make known His truth for your situation. Allow Him to 'yada' you, to make Himself known.

4. Thank the Holy Spirit that He will fill you *with all* joy and peace as you trust Him with this situation.

CHAPTER SEVEN

Joy for Mourning

The Spirit of the Sovereign Lord is on me, because the Lord has anointed me to . . . comfort all who mourn, and . . . to bestow on them . . . the oil of joy instead of mourning.
Isaiah 61:1-3

We were six months into our first year of ministry school, experiencing our first Californian winter. Covid-19 restrictions were in full force, and large gatherings were not allowed inside, so classes had to take place in the revival tents. This didn't make for the most comfortable experience—the fold-out chairs were hard and cold, and the wind would whip and whistle through the tent sides. In an attempt to be a little more comfortable, we started bringing our own camping chairs, along with blankets to wrap ourselves in. While difficult at the time, it makes for a good story now!

On one particular day, we were singing a song about leaning back into Jesus' arms and knowing that He was good, when the worship leader invited us to lean back in our chairs and let the Holy Spirit minister to us. As I did so, I saw a vision of Jesus standing behind me like a hairdresser, washing my hair. He poured an oily substance over my head and with a fine-toothed comb, started combing out the knots. I became aware that He was using the oil of joy to wash my hair and that it was the ashes of grief and mourning that were being combed out. He was so gentle, and it felt incredibly intimate; I gently sobbed and whimpered as the grief I had been carrying came to the surface.

As the vision continued, Jesus started to braid the top part of my hair into an intricate crown. He then set it by placing an old-fashioned hairdryer over my head—the kind you see in the salons in 1970s movies. The heat warmed my head and body, calming my sobs. After several minutes, He lifted off the hairdryer, and my hair grew out from underneath the elaborate crown, extending down to the floor. As I stood from my chair, my hair encompassed me like a garment. I wondered if it was the garment of praise.

Imagine you've had a bad day (or year—or ten!), and someone lovingly washes then tenderly combs and styles your hair, gently cherishing you in every action. There are few acts more intimate than someone touching your hair. During that encounter in the tent, I felt so loved and ministered to, so cleansed. It was a beautiful exchange where the ashes of grief were washed away, and in place, I received a beautiful crown and a new garment.

TOUCHED BY GRIEF

When I decided to write this book, I initially didn't want to write about grief and mourning. My intention was to encourage people to seek after joy at all times—not just during difficulties. I have come to realize, however, that it is impossible to delve into the subject of embracing and living with fullness of joy without recognizing grief and mourning. Sadly, it's something that we all have or will experience in our lifetimes, and in varying ways. It's not only the loss of loved ones that we grieve; it can be the loss of our health or mobility, the loss of independence or a relationship, the loss of our hopes and dreams—the things we have been waiting for that haven't eventuated, perhaps a spouse or child, a ministry or career, a home of our own, or our healing.

JOY FOR MOURNING

But there is hope for when we grieve. In Isaiah 61 we are promised comfort as well as a crown of beauty, the oil of joy, and a garment of praise in exchange for mourning. That day in the revival tents, I experienced the beauty of this gift and felt the joy of it, but it also left me with questions.

The words of Isaiah 61 seem so pivotal—Jesus even drew on them in His first recorded sermon, signaling to us their importance. So much is promised, yet it feels like we seldom see those words fulfilled. Perhaps in part we see the exchange of ashes for beauty, and mourning for joy, and praise instead of a spirit of heaviness. But we don't often see it realized in full. Why is this? Why do people in the church so often mourn just as much and as long as non-Christians when it's not what the Bible offers? Why did it take so long for me to experience this joy, and why are others still mourning after so many years? Perhaps we need to change the way we grieve and what we believe about it, if we are to receive this promised exchange.

Grief is such a difficult topic to discuss because we all respond to loss in different ways and on different timeframes. I want you to hear my heart on this. I don't want it to sound like I am judging others and their grief. As King Solomon said in Ecclesiastes 3, there is a time for everything under heaven, including a time to mourn—and who can tell others how to mourn or how long to mourn for? But I do think that if we believe what God promised in Isaiah 61, then we need to be willing to ask the question: Should there be more freedom in the church when it comes to grief, and should we see a greater exchange of joy for our mourning? If the answer is yes, then we must reconsider how we navigate grieving.

It's quite fascinating to compare the mourning practices in Jewish tradition with how we process our grief now. Amongst other things, the Israelites would wail loudly, beating their thighs to express their anguish, and putting ashes on their head. Sometimes they would go so far as to roll in the ashes or to hire people to wail with them. It was also common to render or tear their clothes and instead wear a dress made of sackcloth, or coarse horsehair. If it was your spouse who had died, you would wear an undergarment made of sackcloth for a month. You would then stay with their body for the week, reading specific psalms over them. One of the things that was often recited was the 'Mourner's Prayer' which focused on God and the hope of the future rather than the feeling of grief. Mourning was given a set timeframe of either seven or thirty days, although some aspects continued for a year depending on how close you were to the person.

This is in stark contrast with what those of us from European backgrounds will have experienced. We tend to mourn quietly, preferring to cry in private and suppress our grief in public. Usually, there is no specific timeframe to our mourning; it is often dependent on when we need to return to work. This lack of space to truly grieve, along with our attempts to keep our emotions under control, can cause people to seek to numb the pain of their loss through medication, alcohol, or drugs.

As I reflected on practices from other times and cultures where widows would wear black to signify that they are in mourning and to remind their community that they need their emotional and financial support, I had to ask myself: *Do we prioritize support for those who are grieving? And do we need to change how we mourn in order to let the soul and body express what they are feeling?* I mean, imagine covering yourself in ashes, or wearing a dress (or a loincloth) of coarse horsehair. Surely the irritation of ash, the discomfort of sackcloth, or the pain of beating our thighs would serve as a helpful expression of the agony our soul's experience. When we find ways to physically express our internal grief, we make way for other emotions to emerge—emotions that can carry us forward and help lift our gaze.

In my mid-twenties when I was working as a physical therapist, the teenage daughter of one of my colleagues was tragically killed by a drunk driver. We were all deeply affected by this, and as we attempted to process what had happened, one of my Christian workmates made a comment that has always stuck with me. She said, "This is something that she will never get over."

At the time I thought it was a fair enough statement. I was still processing the loss of my own father, and had limited life and faith experience. I didn't know how anyone could get over the unexpected loss of a child, of a life cut too short. I couldn't fathom how to process being robbed of the chance to see your child grow up, graduate college, get married, and have the joy of starting their own family—or how to resolve the feelings towards whoever was the cause of all this pain. In my mind, it was one of the worst things imaginable, something you wouldn't even wish on your worst enemy.

More recently, as I have watched friends deal with a similar reality, I have pondered my workmate's statement afresh. *Is it true that some losses are impossible to get over, or is that merely a lie we have been led to believe that no one wants to challenge? Do we not believe it because we haven't seen it?*

SETTING THE CAPTIVES FREE

I don't dream on a regular basis, but I have learnt to take notice when I do. After receiving the promised exchange of joy for myself, I had a confronting dream where I saw people, including some I knew, handcuffed and bound by grief and mourning. It was clear that they were being held in captivity, and in my dream, the Lord spoke to me telling me I needed to set them free by challenging the lies that kept them bound. I found this dream and God's instructions difficult to swallow. I hadn't lost a spouse or child; I didn't know what that felt like. *Who was I to challenge someone else's grief process?* Although I had lost my father too soon (and had felt loss in other ways), it didn't compare to a loss like that. But of course, our losses were never meant to be compared.

As I wrestled with what God was asking me to do and meditated on the verses of Isaiah 61, the Holy Spirit showed me that four groups of people (the afflicted and oppressed, the brokenhearted, the captives, and the prisoners) were *all* held captive by grief—not only the brokenhearted.

The afflicted and oppressed are 'those who are grievously affected mentally or physically, or those who are kept in subservience and hardship'. Many affected by grief are kept subservient to it by the mental and physical toll it takes on their bodies and souls. The same can be true for the brokenhearted. The Hebrew word for brokenhearted, *šāḇar*, carries the idea of 'being maimed by a lion or shattered to pieces like a vase; having your bones fractured; being broken into and robbed; being crushed and destroyed', or 'like the mast of a ship which is broken, experiencing the loss of the wind in your sails, having no direction'. These images so powerfully sum up the impact of grief on a person, and reading them made me physically ache for what my friends who were navigating loss were experiencing.

Captives are like prisoners of war. They are those who have been seized, taken, and held captive, not by what they have done, but by what has been done to them. Grief and mourning are like this; none of us choose it for ourselves—it is the usually a consequence of something that has been done to us or taken from us. There are also those who may be held as prisoners to grief by unforgiveness towards themselves or others, rendering them unable to move past the offense. But the good news is that Jesus came to relieve the oppressed and afflicted, to bind up the broken hearted, and to set free the captives of grief. Isaiah 61 says:

> *The Spirit of the Lord GOD is upon me, because the LORD has anointed and commissioned me to bring good news to the humble and afflicted; He has sent me to bind up [the wounds of] the brokenhearted, to proclaim release [from confinement and condemnation] to the [physical and spiritual] captives and freedom to prisoners, to proclaim the favorable year of the LORD, and the day of vengeance and retribution*

> *of our God, to comfort all who mourn, to grant to those who mourn in Zion the following: To give them a turban instead of dust [on their heads, a sign of mourning], the oil of joy instead of mourning, the garment [expressive] of praise instead of a disheartened spirit.*
> Isaiah 61:1-3 AMP

One of the ways Jesus sets us free is by proclaiming truth. John 8:32 says, "You will know the truth and the truth will set you free." Whether we fall into one or all four of these groups, the lies that we have believed and partnered with must be confronted if we are to be able to receive what God has promised us.

What lies or half-truths have you unknowingly affirmed in respect to grief? Perhaps you are believing that the loss you have experienced is something you can never get over, a burden you will carry forever. Maybe you've decided it's okay to live with grief on earth because you will have joy when you get to heaven. Or perhaps you've believed that you have to cope with grief in your own strength, that it's your job to put off the spirit of heaviness and put on a garment of praise. Maybe you've thought that if you don't grieve long enough or hard enough, it will say something about how much you really loved them . . .

One of the lies I believed, is that it was my responsibility to take off my heavy garment and put on the garment of praise. Growing up in Sunday School we sang a song that told us to "put on the garment of praise, for the spirit of heaviness." But I didn't know the truth; I was unaware that it is the Spirit who does the undressing and redressing! For years I thought I had to *choose* to praise in order to get rid of heaviness, but I was wrong. Much like a lady's maid in *Downton Abbey* who prepares and fits the exquisite clothes to perfection, that is the Holy Spirit's job. This revelation of who is responsible for the exchange of clothing also caused me to think deeper about what He was dressing in me.

WRAPPED IN JOY

Growing up, I had always seen the crown of beauty, the oil of joy, and the garment of praise as three separate things. But as I read different translations of Isaiah 61, I noticed that in some versions there was no 'and'. It was simply written as: the crown of beauty, the oil of joy, the garment of praise. Rather than being a list of three separate things, was this one item described in three different ways? I believe so!

The oil is what is given.

The beauty is what is seen.

The praise is what overflows.

This was not an idea I had heard before, but I found it mirrored in Psalm 30:11-12. There, David writes, "You turned my mourning into dancing; You peeled off my sackcloth and clothed me with joy, that my heart may sing Your praises and not be silent. O LORD my God, I will give thanks forever" (BSB).

Notice the Lord peeled off the sackcloth and clothed him with joy *in order* that he could praise. Neither of these things were done in David's own strength. The praise was the overflow of being wrapped in supernatural joy from the Lord.

The phrase, "spirit of heaviness" refers to the emotional heaviness of grief, or a literal 'spirit' of grief. I have heard it taught that when we believe a lie and partner with it, the enemy gets a stronghold which gives the opportunity for a demonic spirit to attach itself in that area of our lives. Could the cause of prolonged grief be a literal *spirit of grief*? If so, we can command it to leave; we may feel unable to do this in our own strength, but as we partner with the Spirit of God, we will find relief.

One day during worship I felt the Lord tell me to look at the Hebrew word for 'garment' in Isaiah 61:3. I thought this was a strange prompting. It was a garment—what more could there be to it? But as I followed the Holy Spirit's prompting, I was stunned by the revelation He gave.

This reference to a garment in Isaiah is the only time the word *maʽăṭê, is* used in the entire Bible. A *maʽăṭê* is a 'mantle' or 'wrap', but its root word has greater meaning. It means 'to grasp, take with hands, to wrap and to roll'. Is this how God binds up the brokenhearted? By grasping them with His hands, peeling off the sackcloth of grief, wrapping and then rolling them with a mantle of joy?!

I imagined being grasped in the Lord's strong but gentle hands, yielding and relinquishing control to allow Him to remove the sackcloth, and trusting Him to then reclothe—rewrap—me. As I surrendered, I became aware of the closeness of His presence, the warmth, security and comfort that it released. His presence changed my posture; held by God, I was able to stand again. Strength, hope and joy were mine as He bound up my heart and wounds. I couldn't help but overflow in praise at the goodness of God!

This is what the Holy Spirit wants to do for you today. He wants to peel off the sackcloth, the spirit of heaviness, and redress you in the clothing of joy. He gives the crown or countenance of beauty and pours out the oil of gladness so that praise might arise from within you once more.

ACTIVATION

1. Sit with the Holy Spirit awhile. Ask Him to help you identify what you are wearing—is it the sackcloth of grief and mourning, or the garment of praise? Are there any lies you have partnered with that have kept you wearing sackcloth for too long? If so, break your agreement with them!

2. Now, stand up and ask the Holy Spirit, your royal dresser, to undress and redress you, to take away the spirit of despair or heaviness, grasp you with His hands, and wrap and then roll you in the garment of joy and praise. Follow the Holy Spirit's promptings, being sensitive to how He might be inviting you to participate in this process. It may be that He invites you to visualize Jesus taking away the sackcloth and redressing you, or He may ask you to do a prophetic act to symbolize what has taken place.

CHAPTER EIGHT

Sowing in Tears

Those who sow with tears will reap with songs of joy. Those who go out weeping carrying seed to sow will return with songs of joy, carrying sheaves with them.
Psalm 126:5-6

I still remember the day we got the message that a close friend of ours back in New Zealand who had been living with a heart condition for a number of years, had suddenly deteriorated. He had gone to the Emergency Department struggling with his breathing, and over a period of twelve hours his health rapidly declined. We woke to the report that he was in Intensive Care and immediately started to pray for a prompt recovery. As we drove to church, a further update came through that our friend had been placed on a ventilator. Throughout worship we interceded passionately for his healing, but soon after we received the devastating news that his body had given up and the ventilator had now been switched off.

Much to the concern of our children, I began screaming and yelling, "No, no, no, no. This can't be happening!" A cry arose from my gut, *Not on my watch, this is not happening on my watch. This family has had too much devastation and loss!* I promptly recorded a video and shared it with my classmates asking them to join us to pray for his resurrection, something I had never done before. For the next five days Lincoln and I, together with our pastors and friends back home, prayed and believed that God would do what we read of in the Bible—that He would raise our friend from the dead. The day of his funeral came and I lay on the floor of class during worship, messily crying, snot dripping from my nose onto the floor, pleading for God to move in power at this eleventh hour. We had put everything into practice that we had been learning, but much to our disappointment, the funeral went ahead. There was to be no resurrection that day.

We were utterly broken. Our friend's family had already suffered the tragic loss of two of their children—one had died only two years earlier. The loss of their child, along with our own questions as to whether or not God still heals, had been the catalyst for our move to Bethel. Yet here they were, grieving all over again. It all felt so unfair.

Later than evening, after watching the funeral online, a friend posted some thoughts on Facebook about these verses: "Those who sow with tears will reap with songs of joy. Those who go out weeping carrying seed to sow will return with songs of joy, carrying sheaves with them" (Psalm 126:5-6). I was taken by surprise at this, because only three days before getting the initial call about our friend, I had questioned God about those very verses. Struggling to understand what it meant to sow in tears and reap with songs of joy, I had asked the Lord to teach me about it. And now, here was my friend writing on them. His post started with the words: *"Times of mourning are the most difficult times to sow spiritual things into ourselves and others. But it's then that they are most powerful."*

This got me thinking about what I was sowing in my grief. It was so easy to focus on how I was feeling—on my disappointment, my doubt and anger, my disbelief—fixating on what God *hadn't* done, without considering the potential fruit. What would I reap in return? Further grief, or joy? What was going to be harvested from this season?

We are all sowing something, be it positive or negative, intentionally or unintentionally, and as I pondered Psalm 126 and my friend's post I was challenged as to what seeds I would sow during this time. Would I scatter words of encouragement or complaint? Trust or mistrust? Belief or doubt? Contentment or bitterness? Confidence or hopelessness? Faith or fear? I took action and began to intentionally send songs, words of encouragement, Scriptures, and Psalms to my friends back home to strengthen them and focus their attention (and my own) on the truth that *God is good.*

As people grappled with their questions and tried to come to terms with their new reality, I realized why this was such a critical time to sow the truth of God's goodness and faithfulness. Often when people experience loss, they find it hard to trust God. Unable to reconcile their unanswered prayers with what they have believed God is able to do, some give up on church, and sadly, even on their faith. The enemy, knowing they are vulnerable, stays close, ready to pick them off and devour them like the hungry lion he is. If we want to thwart his plans, then these are the times that we need to know how to scatter tear-drenched seeds in order to reap with joy.

As I began to study this passage of Scripture and others, I found that although my initial interpretation about sowing words of encouragement was both biblical and powerful, there was much more to these verses than I had initially understood.

THE BACK-STORY TO PSALM 126

Psalm 126 was written after Israel had returned from exile, but to fully understand the significance of this, we need to go back a little further in their history. Following the peaceful reign of King Solomon during which the first temple was built, the nation of Israel turned away from the Lord in favor of worshiping idols. The nation was then divided by civil war into two kingdoms. Although the nation and the kings were repeatedly warned to turn back to God, most did not listen. Eventually, the northern Kingdom, Israel, was conquered by the Assyrians, and the southern Kingdom, Judah, barely survived.

For forty years the prophet Jeremiah, often referred to as 'the weeping prophet', passionately entreated Judah, cautioning her of the impending captivity that would follow if they did not choose the Lord over their idols, but still the people did not listen. Finally, God raised up the Babylonian King Nebuchadnezzar allowing the Babylonians to invade and besiege Judah. Many men, women and children were killed, and the temple was destroyed. As the city and its surroundings burned, the royal family, officials, and tens of thousands of people were taken captive and exiled to Babylon.

Jeremiah, however, remained in Jerusalem continuing to pray for and minister to God's people. He offered hope to the lost nation, sending word from the Lord to those in exile that unlike the Northern Kingdom, Judah's exile wouldn't be forever. The message he shared with them included the now familiar and often quoted promise from Jeremiah 29:11: "For I know the plans that I have for you, plans for welfare and not for calamity to give you a future and a hope" (NASB). I wonder how those words were received by them? I don't imagine they felt like they had much of a future to look forward to at that time!

Psalm 137 gives us a window into the profound sorrow and despair the exiles felt as they gathered by the rivers of Babylon. Far from the land of promise, they hung their harps on the poplar trees and wept as their captors demanded they sing songs of joy. I don't blame them for not wanting to sing and worship. I wouldn't have wanted to sing for the people who had just destroyed and pillaged my home, killing my friends and family, either. In fact, I would probably have chucked the instruments right at those tormentors. It's not hard to understand why they questioned how they could possibly sing the songs of the Lord while held captive in a foreign land; they probably wondered if they would ever sing songs of praise again.

Yet they did. The Lord redeemed them just as He had promised, just as Jeremiah had told them He would. The Lord moved the heart of King

Cyrus of Babylon to not only let them go, but also to make provision for the rebuilding of the temple. The pain of God's people was not permanent—their circumstances were reversed, and their deliverance was great! As David wrote, "Weeping may last through the night, but joy comes in the morning!" (Psalm 30:5 NLT).

It is at this point in Judah's history that Psalm 126 was penned, acknowledging and celebrating all God had done on their behalf and the joy He had restored to them:

> *When the LORD restored the fortunes of Zion, we were like those who dreamed. Our mouths were filled with laughter, our tongues with songs of joy. Then it was said among the nations, "The LORD has done great things for them." The LORD has done great things for us, and we are filled with joy.*
> *vv. 1-3*

Notice these initial verses are written in past tense. This was a song that they had written previously and now sung in remembrance of the wonder of what God had done for them—seldom was it heard of that a nation returned from exile, but God had made a way for them. Having acknowledged God's past faithfulness, they then started singing in the present tense, followed by a declaration of what God would do in the future:

> *Restore our fortunes, Lord, like streams in the Negev. Those who sow with tears will reap with songs of joy. Those who go out weeping, carrying seed to sow, will return with songs of joy, carrying sheaves with them.*
> *vv. 4-6*

God was faithful to His promise, His word had come to pass. This allowed God's people to respond differently to the new challenges that lay before them. The task of restoring the city and rebuilding the temple and the walls would have been overwhelming—I'm sure it would have been enough to bring them to tears. But as they reflected on what God had done for them, they were able to sing and rejoice because they had faith that God would continue to redeem them. The psalmist's request for God to restore their fortunes like "streams in the Negev" was a vivid picture of the restoration they were expecting. They were believing for an abundant outpouring of God's blessings, and so they declared that they would reap with joy even amongst the tears.

Is this how we sow in tears? By singing prophetically, releasing the words we have been given for the future, and declaring God's faithfulness even while we cry? I had been in danger of 'hanging up my harp' but God was showing me that I needed to learn to sing in the presence of the enemy; to lift my voice even in the midst of my grief.

A NEW WAY OF DOING THINGS

The more I reflected on Psalm 126, the more I sensed that the Israelites had learnt a new way of doing things. Living in the future hope that Jeremiah had prophesied, they could see that God was now bringing them into a redemption story just as He had promised. In Jeremiah 31, God had given them reason after reason to possess hope. Reminding them of His everlasting love for them (v.3), God had promised to build them up again, telling them that they would once again take up their tambourines and go out to dance (v.4). He then said that not only would they dance, but they would also sing for joy as they replanted their vineyards and harvested the crops from their farms (v.5).

This prophesied redemption story would not take place in a foreign land, but in Zion herself as the Lord gathered His people from the ends of the earth and led them back to their home. He promised to make them like a well-watered garden who sorrowed no more (v.12); all the generations would be glad (v.13), and all would be satisfied by the Lord's bounty (v.14). Jeremiah assured them of all this, saying, "Restrain your voice from weeping and your eyes from tears, for your work will be rewarded" (v.16).

Restrain your voice from weeping and your eyes from tears. Could it be that restraining ourselves from prolonged grief is the work we should be doing, the work that will ultimately be rewarded? I think so. I think this might be why, when Jeremiah told them hope lay ahead, he also told them to build houses and plant gardens and marry and increase as they sought the prosperity of the city they had been exiled to (Jeremiah 29:5-7). The work before them was to keep living while they waited for what had been promised to them.

I wonder, if they could go back in time, what they would say to their younger selves? Would they encourage them to pick up their harps and sing joyfully? Would they tell them to meditate on the words of hope that Jeremiah the prophet had spoken to them? Would they change the way they responded at the rivers of Babylon?

Imagine if, instead of their unrestrained weeping, the exiled Israelites had gotten up and sang a joyful song to the Lord their Redeemer, declaring who He is and what He would do, picking up their harps and worshiping the Lord in the presence of their captors, sowing seeds of hope in their distress. Imagine the reaction of the Babylonians. Surely they would have been surprised and intrigued, their curiosity piqued as to who this God was who could enable them to sing under such circumstances. Imagine the seeds that could have been scattered into the minds and hearts of the people of this foreign land. Imagine the potential harvest! How counter-intuitive, how counter-cultural, how powerful.

Now let's make it personal: Imagine how the enemy would respond if in the midst of our grief we got up, picked up our harps, and sang prophetic declarations about our faithful God, about the One who has loved us with an everlasting love and drawn us with unfailing kindness. What seeds would be sown in the lives of those around us as they watch on?

When I was in my dark days of deep distress, I cried, wailed, complained, and questioned; I definitely didn't get up and sing! I didn't even know that that was an option. No one had ever suggested it, let alone demonstrated it. Now don't get me wrong—crying, wailing, questioning and even complaining, are not wrong. As we will discover, these things are an important part of the grieving process that allow us to see joy restored. But I've discovered the power and joy that comes when in the midst of these we also get up and sing prophetically about our Redeemer, the One who brings us back from exile and sends streams in the desert, offering us comfort and gladness instead of sorrow.

~

Our twentieth wedding anniversary happened to fall on the day of our friend's funeral and we were due to go away for a long weekend. Even though we were emotionally exhausted from the week of interceding and didn't feel like celebrating, we made the choice to go away anyway. As Lincoln and I enjoyed the beautiful scenery of the Sonoma Valley wine country, we raised a toast to our friend and his legacy of steadfast faith in the Lord. We declared that even though he wasn't raised from the dead, our faith and the faith of many others was raised, and that one day, resurrections would become commonplace. That weekend, we got up and played our harps, so to speak; we sowed in tears and we reaped in songs of joy.

ACTIVATION

1. What area of your life do you need to release hope into by prophetically singing and declaring the goodness of God?

2. Reflect on a time when the Lord has come through for you. What did He do for you? Remember the joy He brought you and allow it to build fresh faith and expectation within you.

3. Now, 'pick up your harp' and write a song of declaration, asking the Holy Spirit to bring you words and a melody. I know that this activity will be a stretch for many, but I encourage you to give it a go. If you find yourself unable to do it, consider personalizing the words of Jeremiah 31 and speaking or singing them out, or find a song that makes declarations of hope. One of my own favorites is "Fear is Not My Future" by Brandon Lake. However you choose to do it, this is a time to intentionally sow in songs of joy.

CHAPTER NINE

A Pathway Back to Joy

Our hearts ache, but we always have joy.
2 Corinthians 6:10 NLT

In the weeks that followed our friend's death, life was busy, leaving little time and space to process our loss. As part of our studies, we had to go on a mission trip within the states, and it just so happened that these fell immediately after the funeral. With no family in America, the logistics of these outreach weeks were a bit of a juggle for us, and consequently we had decided that it would work best if Lincoln and I went on separate trips. While one of us went off on mission, the other would stay home attending classes and seeing to the responsibilities of the household and children. As it happened, it was my turn to go away first.

You might think the trip would have offered some respite with no children to look after, but let's just say that traveling twelve hours via minivan through two different states, ministering for three days and nights with little to no downtime, and sleeping on a futon in a loungeroom with other students, then packing up to travel back again, was no easy feat, and my middle-aged body did not respond well. By the time I arrived home I was utterly exhausted. But there was no time to catch my breath—I had to pick up the reins at home as Lincoln left for his own mission trip.

Physical tiredness set in and a spirit of heaviness fell on me. Without my husband by my side, I found myself struggling with the school environment. Every song seemed to be about victory; about God being the healer and defeating the grave. I just wasn't in that place. My mind was still saying, "I believe," and I was in full agreement with what I had been learning, but my heart and emotions wouldn't allow me to sing it. I felt too weighed down to continue sowing into myself and those around me.

I was deeply burdened for my friends back home who had experienced too much loss in such a short time, and every day I found myself crying through our times of worship. The days turned into weeks and my classmates were worried about me—so was I. *What had happened to the gladness I had encountered? How was I meant to write this book about joy when it seemed to have left?* I didn't want to end the year in defeat and unbelief, yet I felt crushed to the core. I had never been so convinced of something before or believed so absolutely that God could do the impossible. Only eighteen months ago when our friends' son had died, praying for resurrection had never even entered my mind, and yet this time, I had been sure God would raise our friend from the dead.

I didn't know what to do with this grief. I didn't want to deny it or try to push it down and move on, and in all honesty, I don't think I could have done that even if I had tried. But I also didn't know how to process it, especially in an environment that was all about believing and declaring for the impossible to be done.

The day I got my breakthrough is clearly etched in my mind. It was a Tuesday, and I was sitting in the Redding civic auditorium in the section nicknamed 'third heaven', up in the balcony on the right-hand side. I had just spent the entire forty-five minutes of worship crying, and my red puffy eyes were proof. Dann Farrelly, who was teaching that day, told a joke before starting the class. He carried so much joy and had such a great sense of humor. His infectious laugh always made me want to chuckle along—just not this day. But then he introduced the topic of the Psalms, and began sharing about the different types of psalms, including the psalms of lament. Lament, if you're not familiar with the word, is the process of expressing your grief or regret to the Lord—a process he acknowledged is now a lost art for many Christians.

As he taught on these particular psalms, I felt as if he was reading my mind. Dann verbalized the struggle that it can pose to be in church on a Sunday morning and only hear songs of victory when you are in deep grief or wrestling with disappointment, drawing our attention to Solomon's words in Proverbs where he says, "Like one who takes away a garment on a cold day, or like vinegar poured on a wound, is one who sings songs to a heavy heart" (Proverbs 25:20). He spoke on the tension for the church, pointing out that if we spent our time together singing songs about grief and heartache, everyone would go home depressed and probably never come back.

But the real moment of revelation for me came when he explained that in an environment of faith like the one we were in where we were praying and believing for God to do the impossible, there is 'double grief' when we don't see the miracle come to pass—first, for the loss of the person or thing, and secondly for the miracle that we didn't see happen. It is this second loss, this 'double grief,' that is the reason many people stop praying for the hard stuff. It's as if the disappointment just becomes too much for them.

It was like a lightbulb went off in my head. I wanted to yell, "Yes! That's exactly how I have been feeling—double grief!" I had never resonated with something so wholeheartedly. *Why had I never heard this before in over forty years of being in church?* With so much sadness and difficulty in our world and so many unhealthy ways of coping with it, why doesn't the church teach more about lamenting? Why don't we practice it when it is displayed so often in Scripture? Surely this needs to change if we are to walk in the fullness of all that God has for His people and stem the tide of disillusionment within the church as people grapple with loss and unanswered prayer.

The leader of our ministry school was asked one day, "What is one thing that you would hope every student would know before they left school?" His response was, "Apart from loving God more, loving people, and focusing on God's presence, it would be knowing how to deal with disappointment." One of the common reasons people give for leaving the church and no longer believing in God is when someone they prayed for dies or doesn't get healed. This is why it is so important that we learn how to deal with grief and disappointment in a healthy way, because if we don't (or won't), we risk losing our faith and joy, as well as our expectation for it ever returning. I believe that the lost art of lament is a pivotal key to processing disappointment well.

THE LOST ART OF LAMENT

The word lament means 'to moan, weep, wail, grieve, cry or mourn' and is the process of verbally expressing our deep sorrow, grief, or regret. It is a way we can pray and journal to process our pain with the Lord; it's calling out to God in our distress and asking Him for the help we need. Lament is what differentiates our experience of grief from the world's. As Mark Vroegop once said, "To cry is human, to lament is Christian."

Given the lack of teaching on this topic, you might be surprised to know this, but lament is a major theme in the Bible. It's in Job, the minor prophets, and particularly in the book of Psalms—there's even a whole book dedicated to it called Lamentations. Within the psalms, those dedicated to lament make up the largest category, about one-third of the entire book. When you study these psalms, you see that they either have a corporate or individual focus. Corporate laments deal with situations of national crisis, describing problems faced by all the people of God, whereas individual laments consider the troubles faced by one person. They address issues from unjust physical suffering and illness to alienation and exile, humiliation, injustice and death, and are a good place to go when we need to get real with God about how we feel about our own struggles.

In the psalms of lament, the various dimensions of grief are reflected. They speak to the physical, social, emotional, spiritual and behavioral impact of loss, yet somehow they also infuse our hearts with hope. When we read and meditate on the psalmist's words, leaning into the descriptive imagery revealing their innermost emotions, we learn from their example—they took their pain to God and they left His presence different. And we can too. If we will allow them to, these psalms can provide language for our pain and give us a way of structuring our thoughts.

A CASE-STUDY IN LAMENT

While we often associate King David with his joyful worship and exuberant dancing, he also knew how to lament well. A prolific writer, he penned at least seventy-three of the one hundred and fifty psalms, allowing us to see just how transparent with God he was about his emotions—both when he was walking in God's ways, and when he stepped out into sin and returned in repentance. David wore his feelings and emotions on his sleeve, laying them bare before the Lord, 'yada-ing' with God, allowing himself to be known. No wonder the Bible speaks of him as a man after God's own heart. David allowed himself to be truly *known by the Lord*.

One of my favorite psalms of lament is Psalm 142. I particularly love it in The Message—the contemporary language brings vivid imagery and heightened emotion to David's words, and the psalm itself provides a great example of how we can structure our own prayers of lament.

There are several ways in which the psalmists framed their laments. One method that I think is particularly effective divides lament into four stages: *Turn, Complain, Ask, Trust*. When we add adjectives to these words, the descriptions provide us with the how for each section. I have inserted where each of these sections falls in Psalm 142 in parentheses so you can clearly see David's own process of lament:

[Turn quickly]

I cry out loudly to God,

loudly I plead with God for mercy.

[Complain freely]

I spill out all my complaints before him,

and spell out my troubles in detail:

"As I sink in despair, my spirit ebbing away,

you know how I'm feeling,

Know the danger I'm in,

the traps hidden in my path.

Look right, look left—

there's not a soul who cares what happens!

I'm up against the wall, with no exit—

it's just me, all alone.

I cry out, God, call out:

'You're my last chance, my only hope for life!'

[Ask boldly]

Oh listen, please listen;

I've never been this low.

> *Rescue me from those who are hunting me down;*
>
> *I'm no match for them.*
>
> *Get me out of this dungeon*
>
> *so I can thank you in public.*
>
> **[Trust fully]**
>
> *Your people will form a circle around me*
>
> *and you'll bring me showers of blessing!"*
>
> *Psalm 142 (MSG)*

Turn Quickly

The first step in the process of lament is to turn towards the Lord when we are in pain—and the quicker the better. As David demonstrates, this turning doesn't have to be lengthy or complicated; it can be as simple as stating what David did: "I cry out loudly to You."

However, while this turning can be simple, it's not always easy, nor is it always our first instinct. More often than not, we don't want to feel pain, so we turn to anything that can dull it or distract us from what we are feeling. It's all too easy to withdraw and isolate ourselves—especially with so many vices within arm's reach. Social media and Netflix to distract us; food and chocolate to comfort us, or more destructive vices like alcohol, drugs and casual sex to numb the pain and temporarily fill the void inside.

When David wrote Psalm 142, he had fled Israel in order to escape from King Saul who was trying to kill him—he'd even pretended to be insane to prevent being captured. Cold, isolated and alone, the comforts of palace life had been stripped from him and his future was unknown. Yet in the midst of his fear, he knew to turn to the Lord and cry out. We, too, must learn to quickly turn to the Holy Spirit when we are sad, hurt, or angry. He must be our first, and not last, resort, and the One who we turn to for comfort.

Complain Freely

Once you have turned to the Lord, pour out your complaints, and do it fully and freely. Yes, I said complain, and do it fully! I want you to notice how much time David devoted to complaint: For twelve lines he poured out his grievances before God—twice as many lines as he gave any other section.

There can be a tendency in the church to think that it's not okay to question God. I remember being told by a friend when I was younger that it says in the book of Job that you shouldn't question God. Let's look at the context. In Job chapter 7, Job puts question after question to God, asking Him "Why have you made me your target?" (v.20). God doesn't directly answer Job's questions—in fact, He replies with two chapters of questions of His own. Some have interpreted His response as, *Who are you to question me?* But while God's sovereignty and vastness are implied in His many questions to Job, He never actually tells Job that he isn't allowed to ask his questions.

Over and over, Scripture portrays how people interact with God in difficulties—how they cry and grumble and wrestle and question. Even Jesus asked the Father to take the cup of suffering away from Him when He was destined for the cross (Mark 14:36). Rather than rebuking His people for their doubts and questions, God actually issues an invitation saying, "Come now and let us reason together" (Isaiah 1:18,KJV). God invites us to figure it out with Him—He even offers us a teacher and guide for the journey, the Holy Spirit (John 14:26). If we don't ask God our questions, how can He teach us? And if we won't be honest with Him, how can we maintain our intimacy with Him?

Connection is critical to any relationship. When we don't work through the events and issues that mark our lives, separation can occur. This is evident in the lives of people who are disappointed in or angry with God and have walked away from their faith and fellowship. Don't let this be your story. We have to believe that God has big enough shoulders to deal with our complaints and that He isn't going to kick us out of the family when we have questions for Him. I remember when my husband and I were going through the most difficult point in our lives thus far. I came to a crossroads where I faced a choice: Would I draw near to God or distance myself? I chose relationship. Instead of withdrawing in anger, I called out to God and freely complained, questioning His plans, His ways, even His existence. By doing this, our connection was maintained and even deepened.

You might be tempted to skip this aspect of lament entirely—perhaps you're afraid to acknowledge your pain, or think that it's weak to do so. Maybe religion has told you that if you complain or have questions you mustn't really believe in God. But please don't bypass this step and jump straight to praise. God doesn't want you to hold onto your questions and disappointment and anger. He knows how wearying that is. That's why He invites you to come to Him so that He can relieve you of the weight you have been carrying and give you rest (Matthew 11:28).

I want to encourage you to bring your burdens to God and complain freely—He knows your thoughts anyway, so nothing is gained by pretending that they don't exist. In fact, suppressing our true feelings can lead to stress, physical pain, and even illness. It can also obscure our perspective and keep us from hearing what God is saying about a situation. The very process of pouring out your feelings to the Lord can even be cathartic. I now actually enjoy it! It helps me to sift through my muddled feelings and see things as God does. This was what happened for David too. After twelve lines of complaining his thoughts were clarified and he was able to ask for what he needed.

Ask Boldy

The people of Israel frequently mucked up. The Old Testament is filled with stories of them going against God's laws and worshiping idols, and yet we also see that they repeatedly came to the Lord to ask Him for help. The enemy would have us believe that if we caused our problems then we need to sort them out ourselves. This only isolates us from God's grace. *Remember the prodigal son who spent all his inheritance and went back to ask his father's forgiveness and beg to become a servant in his house?* The father's response was to run towards his son and give him a robe and a ring and put on a feast in celebration. Our heavenly Father longs to do the same. Hebrews 4:16 tells us to "come boldly unto the throne of grace, that we may obtain mercy, and find grace to help in time of need" (KJV). When we come to the Lord boldly and ask Him for what we need, it creates an opportunity for answered prayer.

In Psalm 142, we see that David asked the Lord to rescue him from those who persecuted him, and to bring him out of the 'dungeon' (that cave he was hiding in probably did feel like a dungeon—cold and void of light, with no doors or windows). He knew God was his "only hope for life" and so he boldly and specifically asked for what was needed at that time. As we bring our own requests before the Lord, it is important that we invite the Holy Spirit to minister to us. This is not just an intellectual exercise where we write down or call out our needs; it's an opportunity for the Lord to meet us and provide for us; ultimately, we are in desperate need of *Him*.

If you are anxious and stressed, ask for His peace. If you are in anguish, ask for His presence to bring you comfort. If you are sad and in grief, ask Him to pour out His joy and fill you with hope. If you need His provision, ask specifically for what you need. When I have gone to God and asked Him to comfort me, the Holy Spirit has opened my eyes and I have seen myself sitting on my heavenly Father's knee, and felt myself being pulled into His chest and encompassed in His arms of love. You can experience this same nearness too. So don't be shy, *ask*.

Trust Fully

The purpose of lament is to lead us into greater trust; to get us to the place where we can praise God, proclaiming His promises and declaring the truth of who He is and what He has done and is doing in our lives. Some have called this final step, "Choose to Trust."

Trust is a choice; it is a conscious decision to yield to the Lord. But how do we do this—especially in times of brokenness? We return to the principle of *yāda;* of knowing God and being known by Him. As we connect with the Holy Spirit and He clothes us in joy, praise will overflow. This is not something that we need to try and do in our own strength, nor can we, because the ability to give God praise during times of difficulty is the work of the Holy Spirit in us. He is the One who fills us with all joy and empowers us to keep trusting in the Lord.

One of the common arguments that I have heard against the lamenting process is, "I'm not ready to move on from complaint and request just yet," or, to put it another way, "It doesn't happen that quickly and my heart is not quite there." Learning to trust the Lord is a process and not always a one-time thing—although with the Holy Spirit it can be. We see this gradual journey towards trust in some of the psalms where the psalmist will shift back and forth throughout the various sections, moving from complaint to asking and then back to complaint before finally arriving at trust. This is human nature.

At times we may believe in our minds that God is good and that we can trust Him, but our hearts and emotions haven't yet caught up. That is okay, and often part of the process. The important thing is that we ask God to meet us there. This lag between my emotions and what I know to be true has been my story at times too, but the more I have meditated on the truth of the Word and focused my attention on God's face and who He is, allowing Him to minister to me, the easier I have found it to trust Him fully. I now move more quickly and genuinely into that position.

The practice of healthy lament can help to address the numerous and varied feelings that come with grief, including denial, anger, bargaining or depression, and provide a pathway forward in the grief process. It can lead us towards acceptance and hope, taking us on a journey back to joy as it grows our relationship with the Lord and broadens our experience of Him.

As David discovered, the fruit of lamenting with God is always fresh hope, peace, and joy. Just read the last line he wrote in this psalm: "Your people will form a circle around me and you'll bring me showers of blessing!" (Psalm 142:7 MSG). *I* can't help but wonder if David had a vision or a prophetic picture of that very thing; if through communing with the Holy Spirit he saw God's people once again welcoming him in and circling around him. His words certainly reveal a renewed expectation for his future. There's nothing quite like a prophetic picture which reveals the Father's heart, to reignite your joy!

~

The class on lament was so significant for where I was at in that season, yet many students I have spoken to don't even remember it. God knew what I needed that day, and He beautifully provided it. Since then, I have used this structure to navigate the hard places of my journey with the Lord, and it has helped me return to joy again and again. I pray it will do the same for you.

ACTIVATION

1. Consider something you are grieving or have regret about, and write your own prayer of lament. If you are struggling with putting words to your grief, start by reading Psalms 10, 13, 22, 77 and 88. Once you have written your lament, spend some time analyzing it. *Have you included each of the sections? What sections of the lament structure are missing? Where did you spend the most time in your prayer?*

2. Now consider the four sections of lament in the wider context of your life:

    Turn Quickly

    Do you find yourself turning to substances or habits to help you avoid the pain of grief? Do you run to God quickly, or do you run to Him after you try everything else?

    Complain Freely

    Do you stay stuck in complaint? Are you still complaining about things that happened twenty years ago that haven't been processed or forgiven?

    Ask Boldly

    Do you struggle to ask the Lord for what you need? Why or why not? Do you see Him as a good Father who provides for His children? Is there a lie you are believing about His character or His love for you?

    Trust Fully

    Can you trust the Lord with the situation you have lamented? If not, why? Sit with the Lord and ask Him to minister to you in any areas you have identified. Invite the Holy Spirit to fill you afresh with hope, joy, and peace.

CHAPTER TEN

The Banquet Table

Even though I walk through the valley of the shadow of death, I will fear no evil, for you are with me; your rod and your staff, they comfort me. You prepare a table before me in the presence of my enemies; you anoint my head with oil; my cup overflows.
Psalm 23:4-5 ESV

One of the topics we taught on in the self-esteem course I helped facilitate during my years in New Zealand was resilience. A lady who completed the program reported back on the impact this particular session had made on her, and how during a season of loss she had implemented what she had learnt. She had identified that in order to be more resilient she needed to make herself eat even when she didn't feel like it, so that she could continue to function and be strong for herself and her children.

In the same way, if we want to be spiritually resilient, we need to 'eat' and 'drink' regularly so we can possess the strength to navigate life's challenges well. This is reflected in the picture of our Good Shepherd leading and guiding us in a way that makes space for our needs to be tended to.

I've always loved Psalm 23 and the vivid imagery David uses to describe what it's like to be a sheep with the Lord as our Shepherd. Drawing on his own experience of being a shepherd boy, David writes of the Lord's protection and provision, and His nearness even when life's path takes us through dark valleys. But have you ever noticed what the Shepherd offers us after we have walked through the valley of the shadow of death? A table.

God lays a table for us even while our enemies watch on! It's more than just a table for us to sit at; it's a banqueting feast—one scholar likens it to a six-course dinner! But we can only taste this meal *after* we have come through the shadows, *after* we have journeyed through the darkness and the anguish of the valley. That's when we need nourishment, and that's when we need to regroup and have our wounds tended to so we can continue to journey forward. But what exactly is on offer at this table? And how do we partake of it? Let's take a closer look at some of the imagery in Psalm 23 to discover the answers.

PREPARED TO FEAST

Can you imagine what it must have been like to go on a journey in biblical times? There were no cars, no planes, no trains or buses—a donkey would have been the most likely mode of transportation, and even then there was often only one per family. Traveling would have been a long, dangerous, and dirty affair. You'd arrive at your destination exhausted, your feet sore and blistered from days of walking and your muscles tired and aching from carrying your belongings. If you were headed to a celebration, it's likely that in your travel-weary state you would not have felt much like feasting with your hosts—you'd have wanted to get cleaned up first and catch your breath.

But just as there was no modern transportation, there were no modern conveniences—no hotels or showers for you to freshen up before heading out. Instead, you were reliant upon the hospitality of your host.

One of the first things a host would do for their arriving guests was to anoint them. Fragrant perfumes were mixed with oil and used to anoint the guests' heads, washing away the dust, while soothing and refreshing the weary traveler and reviving them for the party. This ancient custom was reserved for the most esteemed dinner guests and is likely what David had in mind when he said, "You anoint my head with oil" (Psalm 23:5). The oil of anointing represents both the Holy Spirit *and* the oil of gladness, and it is available to be poured out on you, washing away the 'dust' of disappointment, soothing any wounds, and bringing you comfort, love, peace, joy, and strength. But sadly, not all God's 'guests' allow themselves to be tended to in this way.

A. W. Tozer said, "It is a solemn thing, and no small scandal in the Kingdom, to see God's children starving while actually seated at the Father's table." Are these children that Tozer speaks of unable to eat and drink at the table because they lack the energy? Are they too tired and burdened from their travels? Do they know they should feed themselves with the Word, but lack the strength to eat of it?

How often in life have we also felt this way? The journey has been hard and sometimes treacherous, and we haven't had the energy or desire to join the festivities. In order to consume what has been prepared for us and freely participate in the celebrations, we need to first be refreshed by the fragrant oil of the Holy Spirit. We need to spend time with our 'host' and allow Him to soothe and revive our weary bodies and hearts. As an esteemed guest, your good shepherd wants to fellowship with you; He wants to anoint your head with oil so you can come to the table feeling refreshed and hungry.

Interestingly, the same oil that would have been used to anoint the invited guests' heads, would have been used to anoint those of the sheep. I used to think that the symbolism of the shepherd stopped in Psalm 23 after verse 4, when the table was set. But there is dual symbolism in these final verses. Shepherds would prepare what was also known as a 'table', going ahead of the sheep to prepare a suitable resting spot on the mountain where they could care for them as they came up and out of the valley. And there, they would anoint them.

Oil was used frequently in the care of sheep to protect them from flies, scabs and injury during the mating season. In the summer months, nasal flies were especially problematic. These little flies would buzz about the sheep's head, attempting to lay their eggs on the warm mucosa of the sheep's nose. If successful, small worm-like larvae would hatch within a few days, work their way up the nasal passages into the sheep's head, and burrow into the flesh causing immense irritation, severe inflammation, and sometimes blindness. This was incredibly painful for the sheep, and they would try to relieve themselves of the pain by beating their heads against trees, rocks, posts or brush. In extreme cases they would even kill themselves. In their agitation, they would toss their heads up and down for hours or drop from sheer exhaustion after frantically stamping their feet and running erratically in an attempt to get away from the flies and avoid the distressing pain. Ouch, sounds horrid, doesn't it?

By anointing their heads with fragrant oil, the flies would be repelled, as were microscopic parasites that were often spread through a flock by sheep rubbing their heads up against each other. Left untreated, these parasites would cause irritation and sometimes scabbing. In addition to warding off the bugs, the oil also helped to heal any wounds they had inflicted. It also minimized injuries during mating season when the rams fought for possession of the ewes. They would strut and fight furiously for favor, so to reduce the likelihood of them being killed or maimed in the process, the shepherd would smear oil on their heads so that the rams would glance off one another when they came into contact.

When we are plagued by the enemy's advances; when he tries to irritate and distract us and his lies are buzzing around our heads unsettling us and causing disunity within the flock, we need the oil of joy. We must refuse to allow our weariness to keep us from our Shepherd, but instead draw near and ask Him to anoint our heads so that we can experience His healing and protection, and be refreshed to partake of the table He has so lovingly set for us.

THE BANQUET TABLE

DEVOURING AND DELIGHTING

The Good Shepherd has prepared a table, a lavish banquet, for us. But it's not a meal that we have to eat alone. Rather, we are invited to sit with Him—to feast *with Him* at the table while our enemy watches on. Yes, the enemy may be close, and he may be trying to intimidate us, but our Shepherd is even closer. So let's not be shy; let's joyfully eat what He has placed before us.

In Jeremiah 15:16, the prophet Jeremiah says, "When your words came, I ate them; they were my joy and my heart's delight." As a prophet to Judah, Jeremiah shared God's messages with the Israelite people. A fair amount of the time, the people didn't listen, but Jeremiah did. He recognized the strength and joy they brought when he meditated on them and ingested them—some translations even say he *devoured* them.

The 'word' here can refer to a speech or message, advice or counsel, a promise, or the Word of God itself. What a privilege that we get to consume the advice and counsel of the Lord, feasting on the promises of God and gaining strength from what He says to us. We get to sit and eat with the Shepherd who converses with us through the Bible (*logos* words) and offers revelation from the Holy Spirit (*rhema* words). This is what He offered to do for the Israelites when they went into exile. Through Jeremiah, He gave them promise after promise, message after message that would have given them strength, had they 'eaten'. Let's learn from their mistake and take the sustenance that God is offering us.

FEASTING ON THE PROMISES

In my younger years I experienced a lot of rejection, and because of this I lacked confidence. My self-esteem was low and it was as though there was a shadow over my identity. I recognized that I needed to reject the lies I believed about myself and replace them with the truth. So, for a whole year, I carried a card with Psalm 139:13-14 written on it: *"For you created my inmost being; you knit me together in my mother's womb. I praise you because I am fearfully and wonderfully made; your works are wonderful, I know that full well."*

I not only constantly read these verses, I also memorized them, meditating on God's thoughts towards me and ingesting their truth. I did this until I could declare "I know this full well" with conviction. I did the same when my husband was off work, depressed and in constant pain for four years. When things looked hopeless, I continually fed myself with God's promises for our future, meditating on the truth that He had a plan for us, that His heart was to prosper us and not to harm us, that He would give us hope and a future (Jeremiah 29:11).

But it's not only Scripture that we get to chew on. We can also chew on the prophetic words that we have been given, even if they aren't currently evident. Over eighteen years ago, I heard the Lord tell me through Scripture that I would be a speaker—then, at a prophetic conference, I was told I was going to be a 'generation changer'. Neither of these things looked remotely possible in the natural. I was an introvert, in a small church, in a small city, in a dead-end job. I had little favor and very little influence. Yet I have held onto those words, reminding myself of them often and declaring them aloud. I didn't need to do this in my own strength—the Holy Spirit reinforced my words with His voice and His presence. He has built a confidence in me that God's word will not return empty but will accomplish what He desires and achieve the purpose for which He sent it (Isaiah 55:11).

I encourage you to feast on both the *rhema* and the *logos* word; the promises of God and His character, the stories of when He came through, when battles were won, when He provided, the healing power of Jesus, the availability of the Holy Spirit, the prophetic, past and present testimonies—the six-course banquet is available. Consume it, devour it, memorize it, meditate on it, chewing on the cud, go over and over it, just like a sheep does, absorbing every little bit of nutrition from it. It will bring you joy and strength.

THE BANQUET TABLE

DRINKING AT THE TABLE

If you've ever ordered a tasting menu, you'll know that each course is paired with just the right wine. After all, a good feast is as much about the drinks as it is the food. And God is not stingy when it comes to portions or supply—He makes our cup overflow, or as some translations put it, "my cup runneth over" (Psalm 23:5 KJV).

This verse isn't usually associated with drinking, but rather with the abundant blessings that the Good Shepherd pours into our lives. However, the Hebrew word translated as 'runneth over' comes from the root word *rāvâ*, which means 'to be saturated, to drink one's fill, to be drunk, to be intoxicated, to drench, to soak, to water abundantly'. In the earlier Greek Septuagint, verse 5 reads as, "thy cup cheers me like the best wine" or, "my chalice that inebriates me". The blessings that are poured out to us are meant to cheer us and intoxicate us like wine!

In times of immense grief and stress many people turn to alcohol to dull their pain, lift their spirits, and give them some resemblance of happiness. I can completely understand why people would indulge in drink in order to feel some relief, even if just for a short time. Even King Solomon wrote, "give wine for those who are in anguish" (Proverbs 31:6), and in an ancient Jewish tradition called 'the cup of consolation', alcohol would be sent to those in mourning (Jeremiah 16:7). However, while this tradition may provide some immediate relief, we all know the long-term consequences and the destruction alcohol dependency can lead to. What if instead we offered a safer, cheaper, healthier alternative that brings the same lightness (without the hangover!), and whose path leads to life and freedom? *What if we offered the way of the Spirit?*

Ephesians 5:18 tells us not to get drunk on wine, as it leads to debauchery, but to be filled instead with the Holy Spirit. Similarly, Zechariah 10:7 speaks of the hearts of God's people being glad *as with wine*, and the psalmist wrote that, "When anxiety was great within me, your consolation brought me joy" (Psalm 94:19). What if the consolation God offers us is the filling of the Holy Spirit and the joy that He offers? What if this is what the church is currently missing?

Now, I'm fairly confident that the wider church would discourage sending alcohol to help someone drown their sorrows, yet many also speak out against the alternative of hearts being consoled and made glad by the Holy Spirit. Being under the influence of the Holy Spirit—or, for lack of a better term, being 'drunk in the Holy Spirit'—is where people display behaviors similar to those of being drunk on alcohol. The effects might range from being slightly merry or 'tiddly', becoming happy and joyful, to being more 'intoxicated', dancing on the tables, stumbling, falling over, and even shaking and laughing hysterically on the ground. I have experienced each of these manifestations. Sometimes it's been like just having half a glass, while other times it's been as though I have consumed a full bottle or even a large carafe of the finest vintage. What if what Jesus did in the physical, making the most exquisite wine available to the wedding guests (John 2), we now have access to in the spirit? What if He truly has saved the best for last and has given us the wine of the Holy Spirit to wash away our grief, release tension, shake off disappointment, and fill us with joy?

Sadly, many people look in judgment on those who have tasted this sweet wine, without even experiencing it for themselves. They accuse people of wanting attention, wonder about the point of it, and even question the origin of such behavior. In my younger days I too laughed and even pointed at people who were filled with joy and danced with passion before the Lord; I thought it was weird. Yet I never stopped to ask those people about what had happened and what God had done in the process. It wasn't until I experienced it for myself that I understood it.

I can truly say that the joy of the Lord and being 'drunk' or intoxicated in the Spirit, has changed me—and people have noticed. When I returned to New Zealand after my second year of study, people said things like,

"You went away as a girl and you've come back as a woman," or "You're so bold and confident now," and, "You're much more bubbly and free!"

If you aren't sure about these things, my advice is to go and ask those who have encountered the Holy Spirit in this way to share their testimony. From the outside it can look ridiculous and messy, but often people are being set free from anxiety, depression, mental health conditions, addiction, self-hatred, PTSD, fear of man, as well as experiencing physical healing and other miracles. I have heard many testimonies of the freedom received while 'drunk' and laughing on the floor.

Another objection is that the church won't be able to get anything done if we are 'drunk' all the time—well, in my experience the opposite has been true. You wouldn't believe how much of this book has been inspired as the Lord hit me with joy, the number of scriptural revelations I have received while 'under the influence', and the boldness and confidence that has come to ask questions and challenge beliefs while 'out cold' on the floor. There is so much power, freedom and revelation that can come through Holy Spirit joy and laughter. We do not need to worry that these expressions of His infilling will waste time.

God is the inventor of laughter and happiness, and even now He is singing and dancing as He releases joy over us. What if He just wants to dance, and laugh and sing *with* us? It's like when a friend starts to laugh and they catch your eye, causing you to laugh too—you try to stop but when you look at them again it just makes you laugh even more. Laughter is so catchy, and God wants us to catch His.

I wish I had learnt the power of Holy Spirit joy and laughter years ago. For so long I needed my spirit to be lifted, but I didn't even know that I did. Now that I have experienced greater levels of joy, I want others to experience it too. I believe that if we actively encouraged 'Holy Spirit joy' in the church, we would see anxiety reduced, the heaviness of grief lifted, and freedom and gladness restored to broken hearts.

Can you imagine the devil's frustration if we collectively accepted the Shepherd's invitation to join Him at the table? Imagine his irritation when, instead of being consumed by fear and grief, God's people are filled with the truth of His Word and the power of the Holy Spirit, laughing and singing and dancing with our King as we declare with David, "Surely goodness and mercy shall follow me all the days of my life." (Psalm 23:6 KJV). This goodness is available to us right now, the table is set, the invitation is sent; we just need to sit at the table and consume the feast, devouring and delighting and drinking deep. Will you join me there?

∼

For six weeks I lamented and processed the grief of our friend's passing, and as graduation neared, I was still heavy-hearted. I found it difficult to cope with the festivities going on around me—I didn't feel like taking part, and I definitely didn't feel like dancing. I felt like a kill-joy as I struggled to put on a happy face for those around me.

During graduation week, we were commissioned to go out and live what we had been taught. Lincoln and I arrived at the civic auditorium early in the morning. As we entered, I was aware that the atmosphere felt weighty with the presence of the Lord. It was so tangible, something I had not experienced to that degree before. I had known the heaviness of God's presence on me before, but nothing like this—it filled the entire room. I enjoyed the atmosphere, conscious that the Holy Spirit was close, and within fifteen minutes of arriving, before the ceremony had even started, I realized I already felt happier. A shift had taken place, and I now wanted to join in the festivities, something I hadn't wanted to do for weeks.

No one had prayed for me, I hadn't sung any songs, I had simply walked with the Lord and He had led me through the valley of the shadow of death, through the heaviness. And now, He had anointed me afresh with the oil of gladness and it was starting to overflow again.

ACTIVATION

1. Are you weary from a treacherous journey? Think of yourself as the distinguished guest that you are, the one whom the Good Shepherd wants to anoint. Close your eyes and imagine Him pouring fragrant oil onto your head, bringing you comfort and refreshment.

2. Now that you are ready to sit at the table, identify an area where you need to feast on His truth. Feed yourself with the Word, finding Scriptures on this topic and recalling and declaring any prophetic words that you have been given.

3. Once you are 'full', using your sanctified imagination, imagine yourself with a large cup overflowing with the sweet wine of the Holy Spirit. Drink up, take a sip, down a cup, pour it over your head so you are saturated. Do this daily, allowing your Good Shepherd to build resilience and enable you to walk the path He has for you with joy.

CHAPTER ELEVEN

Shouting for Joy

Shout for joy to the Lord, all the earth. Worship the Lord with gladness; come before him with joyful songs.
Psalm 100:1-2

It was one of our final worship sessions for the year and everyone around me was caught up in passionately praising the Lord. Some were singing with their hands raised high, while others danced and leapt, waving their scarves in the air as they joyfully shouted. It was quite the scene to observe. People here were so expressive in their praise, and the environment we were in actively fostered this atmosphere of rejoicing. They seemed to know the strength that is found in the joy of the Lord and how much they needed it.

With holidays looming, I started to reflect on how far the Lord had brought me, asking Him to show me how to maintain the joy I now possessed for the long-term. My levels of joy had fluctuated over the past nine months even in this radically joyful environment, and I didn't want to go back to who I had been before coming to America. I didn't want this newly-discovered happiness to wane, or worse, disappear, as I transitioned into different surroundings. We were going away for an extended summer break and would eventually be returning to New Zealand permanently. *How would I maintain a cheerful countenance and the outward expression of praise there?*

Traditionally, New Zealanders aren't known for their exuberance or their overflowing emotions. Generally speaking, we're known for being resourceful people with a good work ethic, a relaxed attitude, and an easy-going nature—some say we're so laid back we're almost lying down. This attitude is often reflected in the way we express ourselves in church, where even raising a hand in worship could be considered extreme in many congregations.

I was worried that once I was back in that setting I might find myself losing joy or low on joy again. More to the point, *what should I do*, once I was immersed in that environment, one that didn't actively encourage or foster joy?

Then the Holy Spirit answered me: "Shout *for* joy and sing His praises."

It was like a light came on. The Holy Spirit had intentionally emphasized the word *for*, and in so doing, had given me a tool that I could use whenever I needed to get my joy back. I stopped worshiping and asked the Lord some more questions. I needed Him to clarify this strategy: *Was He saying I should literally shout for joy, to get joy? That I could summon joy by shouting?*

As I meditated on His answer, I found myself picturing a lone army officer whose troops have scattered in the chaos of battle. He shouts to them, calling them to attention, summoning them to rally and draw near. I could see myself doing this on my own at home whenever I felt despondent or overwhelmed by grief or loneliness, literally shouting and summoning the Spirit of Joy, the One who is all joy, to draw near and rally around.

I knew what it was to shout for joy in a corporate environment, but I wanted to see if it would work in an individual setting too. I knew that I had to try this out; I decided to do an experiment to see if shouting for joy did indeed bring me more joy.

THE JOY EXPERIMENT

The summer holidays presented the perfect opportunity for me to conduct my experiment. Because of our visa regulations we were unable to stay in the States, but nor were we able to return home. New Zealand's borders were closed even to citizens due to strict Covid-19 measures—some of the tightest restrictions in the world. Mexico was the cheapest and most straightforward solution we could find, so we decided to spend the summer there. Away from the environment we had grown accustomed to, I was ready to see if this Holy Spirit-inspired idea would work.

I was determined to get on the front foot and prophylactically shout for joy to maintain my happiness. I knew that we would be in a heavy spiritual atmosphere and that the isolation of holidaying on our own for so long a period would leave me vulnerable to feeling lonely and homesick. So, I made a plan, deciding to shout and sing for joy for at least ten minutes each morning for the first two weeks, no matter where we were situated. I was astonished by the results.

Usually I wasn't a morning person, needing to sit quietly and have a coffee before taking my time to get moving. But after two songs of rejoicing to the Lord (which I couldn't seem to get through without also dancing), I felt invigorated; my mind was clear and focused, and my soul was lighter. I would even go so far as to say I felt like a morning person. Throughout our holiday, whenever I felt sad, heavy, isolated or just a bit down, I would simply worship the Lord, summoning joy. At the end of this trial the experiment had been so successful that I concluded this couldn't just be a one-off; it needed to become a way of life. Since our time in Mexico, I have continued to practice shouting for joy—not daily anymore, but just as the need arises.

The following summer I found myself back in New Zealand and back in the environment I was so fearful of returning to. Living in a less-than-exuberant culture and attending more reserved churches was hard, but to add insult to injury, everywhere I turned there seemed to be somebody dying or afflicted with cancer—and not just the elderly, but those my age. People had little hope for healing, let alone resurrection, and we found that many believers struggled to have faith for the miraculous.

This was the real test of whether this experiment would work: Would this technique the Holy Spirit gave me continue to be effective when all the conditions were against me? I'm glad to report, yes it was. On the days where I felt heavy, I purposely got up to shake off the weight that I felt, putting on lively worship music and shouting for joy as I danced, sang, and summoned the Spirit of Joy. This lifted my spirits, shifted the atmosphere, changed my countenance, and joy did in fact return. But God wanted me to take this experiment even further; He wanted me to include others in it.

While we were in New Zealand, some friends asked me to come and share with their small group. They were aware I was writing a book on joy and were interested to hear what I had been learning. In our absence, each one of them had gone through various trials, and as they shared what they had gone through, they expressed their need for more joy and their desire to have what I had. So, I decided that phase three of my experiment was to try shouting for joy with them.

It was school holidays, but they were still determined to meet—even with a houseful of children in the next room who frequently interrupted us. I began by sharing some of my journey of encountering supernatural joy and how it had changed me. Then I described the experiment I had completed, and how God had led me to shout for joy while singing His praises. I wish you could have seen the look on their faces when I told them that that was what we would be doing! There was shock, surprise, and even fear, upon hearing that we would all be shouting, singing, crying, shrilling, and dancing in my friends' living room that afternoon.

With some hesitation, my poor New Zealand friends reluctantly agreed to give it a go. We all got up off the comfy lounge chairs, everyone looking at each other—I'd say they were feeling a bit stupid, but they gave it a go anyway. I put on an upbeat worship song and instructed them to shout for joy, sing, dance, jump, and let loose. They did it in true Kiwi-style, pared-back, half-volume, and with very little dancing, but we shouted and sang God's praises anyway. By the end of the first song we were all chuckling away, and despite their discomfort, they confessed to feeling invigorated, lighter, and more energetic, and they all felt a level of joy that they hadn't experienced for some time.

What is it about shouting aloud in the context of praise that creates the change and brings the shift in ourselves and in the atmosphere? Why had I seen such a positive impact on myself and my friends?

The Power of Singing and Shouting

In Psalm 100, the language of the original text conveys a much deeper meaning than our English words can fully capture. In verse 1, the Hebrew word *rûa'* is used for the phrase "shout for joy." The connotation is much stronger than just a joyful cry, it signifies 'a signal for war, a trumpet blast, a shout in triumph, applause'. It can even refer to an exuberant response when something is destroyed. When we shout for joy, we are fighting in the spirit realm and waging war; it is a sound of triumph as we declare the enemy is destroyed. What power there is in our shouts!

This power is demonstrated time and again throughout Scripture. Take for example the story in Joshua 6 where Joshua and the Israelites shouted as they came to the end of their seven-day march around the walls of Jericho. These were no flimsy walls! The city of Jericho was surrounded by walls that were nine meters tall (thirty feet) and four meters deep (thirteen feet). And yet, with one exuberant, united, corporate shout of triumph, these mighty walls came crashing down!

Again, in 2 Chronicles 20 we see a similar battle plan unfold. There,

Jehoshaphat appointed men to lead the army into battle, not with a show of weapons or physical strength, but with shouting, and songs of praise to the Lord. As their cry of triumph rang out, the Lord Himself intervened. We read, "the Lord set ambushes against the men . . . and they were defeated" (v.22). The Israelites did not even need to raise their weapons. The only thing left for them to do was to reap the rewards of the goods left on the battlefield. Their battle cry was so effective in the spiritual realm that they had no need to engage in the fight at all!

One of the other Hebrew words translated as "shout for joy" in Scripture is *ranan* meaning 'to overcome, to cry out, shout for joy, give a ringing cry, sing out, sing for joy, rejoice'. When we consider these meanings, we see that the two actions of shouting for joy and singing God's praise are connected.

Through the tribe of Judah, God demonstrated how shouts of triumph and songs of praise work together. The first of the tribes of Israel, their name means 'worship or praise Jehovah'. Whenever the Israelites went to war, Judah was always sent out into battle first. This is a prophetic picture for us, teaching us that when we are faced with battles, we, too, must begin with worship.

We see this approach in the story of Paul and Silas when they were imprisoned after casting out a demon from a female slave. As they prayed and sang praises to the Lord, He fought for them, sending a sudden violent earthquake that shook the foundations of the prison and caused the doors to fly open and everyone's chains to come loose. Their singing preceded their deliverance. Talk about the power of praise! And let's not forget David who would play the harp for King Saul to help him relax whenever he was troubled by an evil spirit. His worship caused the evil spirit to leave, releasing Saul from this bondage.

Both of these accounts remind us that our shouts, our singing, crying, and rejoicing affect the spiritual realm far more than we are aware.

The Natural Effects of Singing

Singing not only shifts the spiritual atmosphere, it also benefits our physical and mental health. Some of the positive impacts of singing include a reduction of stress hormones such as adrenaline and cortisol, and an increase to our 'feel good' hormone, dopamine. In turn, endorphins are released, leading to reduced pain and improved mood. Singing also strengthens our immunity by boosting our immunoglobulin levels. Who would have thought simply singing could make such a difference?!

All these benefits are amplified when people dance or rhythmically drum, and they increase further when done in a group—singing *together* makes a difference. Interestingly, the gains are much greater when singing along to music rather than just listening to it.

I've personally noticed the difference singing can make to our mental well-being. Music helps to shift our thoughts off of our problems—this is especially true when the songs are filled with biblical promises and remind us of who God is and what He can do. It's Philippians 4:8 in practice—through song, we are thinking about whatever is true, noble, right, pure, lovely and admirable. I suppose that's what my friends and I were doing that day, focusing on the One who is noble, right, pure, and lovely as we shouted and rejoiced in Him.

RETURNING TO JOY (AGAIN AND AGAIN)

I remember the first English lesson I did with my then ten-year-old during Covid lock-down, when I suddenly had to become the teacher. The topic was prefixes, something neither one of us knew anything about. I had to google it, learning that prefixes were letters put in front of a word in order to form a new word. Our church had just finished a fast with the theme refocus, so I remember the prefix 're', meaning 'to return, turn back, or again', standing out to me at the time.

The word 'rejoice' carries the same prefix. To rejoice, therefore, means 'to return to joy, turn back to joy, or, joy again'. When we shout for joy, when we sing God's praises, rejoicing in Him, we are returning joy to God, but we are also turning back to joy, to the One who is the source of joy.

RELEASING AND FILLING

The Holy Spirit had opened my eyes to see the role that shouting and singing play in Scripture, and what returning to joy does in the spiritual realm.

When we shout for joy, we are raising a battle cry against the enemy of grief, loneliness, worry and stress, or whatever is weighing us down. As we shout, we wage war, calling out to the troops, the angels, to rally around us and fight for us in the spiritual realm. As we release shouts of triumph, we are declaring that the enemy is destroyed.

When we give God our adoration and thanks, singing His praises, God inhabits that praise (Psalm 22:3). The Holy Spirit is ushered in, and joy enters with Him. As we return over and over again to joy, shouting and singing and rejoicing in the Lord's presence, we give out, but find ourselves filled up in the process. Having released all our joy, we are filled back up to overflowing. What a blessing.

~

As I have shared my journey of discovering greater joy in the Lord, I have started hearing more testimonies of people receiving freedom, through joy received during worship. Just this week two women told me of times during worship where joy welled up in them, bubbling up inside and releasing one of depression and the other from the fear of man. Our shouts, and our songs of praise and worship, have the power to do more than simply release joy in our own lives—they also have the ability to unlock the chains of others.

I remember going on a mission trip to India many years ago in my mid-twenties. Although we were there to do physical work, we were also asked to minister in church services. As part of this, we had prepared some songs to sing as a group, but the contrast in the style of worship between our songs and theirs was huge. They danced and jumped, playing tambourines and instruments, singing as loudly as humanly possible to express their love to the Lord. Our songs were sedate, almost melancholy in comparison, with no one in the group barely tapping a toe. I think the audience didn't know quite how to respond. We went there to minister to them, but they showed us what it looks like to worship God with abandon.

What does your church congregation sound like on Sunday morning—or at any other time, for that matter? Are you rejoicing? Shouting? Releasing a war-cry? Letting out ringing cries of triumph, trumpet blasts, or songs of praise? Are you knocking down walls or shaking foundations in the spirit? Imagine if we *did* sound like that. Wouldn't it be great if Sunday morning church was more lively than the Saturday night concert or game, if we cheered, applauded, and expressed our praise, with exuberance!

What if we all learnt to collectively *shout for joy*?

I believe that if we can embrace this lesson, we will see people experience the reality of what we so often sing about. The chains of grief will fall off, and the captives and prisoners will be released from their bondage; there will be freedom and liberty. Let's get good at shouting for joy!

ACTIVATION

Conduct your own 'joy experiment'. Every morning for the next week, get up and put on an upbeat worship song. I use an oldie but a goodie, "Shout to the Lord" because it has a line that says, "I sing *for joy."* Take this practice into your day, and whenever you are feeling a bit flat, take two minutes and shout for joy, then watch the spiritual atmosphere shift!

CHAPTER TWELVE

Joy Thieves

The thief comes only to steal and kill and destroy. I have come that they may have life, and have it to the full.
John 10:10

My family has intolerances to wheat and salicylates, natural food preservatives found in many foods, but when I was younger, we didn't know this, and it had a huge impact on my childhood. I remember how every Easter I would end up in bed due to the severity of my symptoms—not exactly how any kid wants to spend a weekend that is meant to involve a lot of fun and chocolate! My symptoms were wide-ranging, including headaches, sinus problems, puffy eyes, sore joints, achy tight muscles, and brain fog. But they weren't only physical, they also affected my moods—my emotions were flat, and the constant sickness left me feeling isolated from others. Once I'd eaten something containing one of these ingredients, there was nothing anyone could do to make me feel better; I just had to wait for the food to get out of my system. Until then, I was held to ransom by my own body.

My diagnosis of endometriosis in my twenties also affected my digestive system, and I went through a period where I was extremely exhausted; I struggled to get through the day, and at times had to go home to take a nap before returning to my shift. I would go to bed tired, sleep twelve hours, and still wake feeling debilitated. When I'm exhausted, I cry—so let's just say I cried a lot in that season! I just didn't feel like myself and I certainly didn't feel like I had the energy of a twenty-five-year-old.

The doctor wanted to put me on antidepressants, but I declined. It's not that I don't agree with their use when they are needed—I simply felt that I wasn't depressed; rather, I felt physically depleted. Shortly afterwards I was referred to a specialist who noted that my Vitamin B12 levels were rather low and could be the cause of how I was feeling. He promptly prescribed regular B12 injections, and within two weeks it was as though I was a new person—I was full of energy and the tears had stopped. The injections revitalized my body and my joy!

My joy was depleted as a result of what was taking place in my body—the issue was physical, not spiritual. While it is true that our enemy the devil prowls around like a lion looking for someone to devour (1 Peter 5:8), it is also possible that as Christians we get too focused on the spiritual aspect of our joylessness. *What if we focused just as much of our attention on the body and soul?* Paul taught that we are triune beings, praying that not only our spirit be kept blameless, but also our body and our soul (1 Thessalonians 5:23). If we want to guard our joy, then we need to start caring for all aspects of our being, recognizing that the enemy is out to steal, kill, and destroy everything.

In these next sections, I want to share very practically about some of the 'joy-thieves' that have been present in my own journey. It is by no means an exhaustive list, but my hope is that they will help you to recognize some of the enemy's tactics in your own life so that you can walk in greater joy.

PHYSICAL THIEVES

In God's original design, sickness and death had no place. When He first made Adam and Eve in His image, they were created in perfect health—it wasn't until the devil came into the Garden of Eden and lied to them, deceiving them into eating the forbidden fruit, that sickness and death entered into the world. From the beginning, the enemy was a thief. But as Jesus declared, He came to restore to us abundant life (John 10:10). Being aware of some of the physical issues that impact our joy levels can help us to lay hold of that life.

Hormonal Imbalances

Hormonal imbalances can affect both men and women at various points in their lives, and, left untreated, greatly impact their levels of joy. I experienced this after giving birth to our daughter in my thirties when for the three days before my period was due, I would be hit with intense pre-menstrual syndrome (PMS). I would find myself crying for no reason at all, and felt anxious about doing things I would normally have no problem with. I knew in my head that I would be fine in just a few days, yet I couldn't stop myself from sobbing. After three months I recognized it for what it was, got my hormones tested, and was prescribed progesterone cream which shifted all the symptoms and evened my emotions out. Now joy stood a chance!

Nutritional Deficiency

Another common issue is nutritional deficiencies. With our modern processed diets, we simply don't always get everything we need from our food—as I discovered in my forties. I was going through yet another time of feeling a bit flat and lacking that get-up-and-go energy, and my twin sister, who is a biochemist and natural health practitioner, completed a test on me called an oligoscan, which evaluates minerals and toxic metals in the blood. She found that I was lacking in a number of minerals and prescribed me several supplements. But there was one she chose not to give me—despite being low in lithium, she left it off the list, as I wasn't suffering from depression. After several months of seeing no improvement, however, I sensed the Holy Spirit prompting me to order the supplement, and within a matter of days of taking it, I felt happy and energetic. I had never had such a quick improvement with any supplement before—I was so thankful for the Holy Spirit's prompting.

Stress Levels

One of the topics we covered in the self-esteem courses I ran for women was about how we approach stressful situations: Do we have a tendency to *react* to the difficulties in our lives, or do we *respond* to them? So many factors can cause us to go to pieces, including how we feel physically and mentally. Many of our participants were multi-tasking mothers who put everyone's needs ahead of their own. We taught them the acronym HALTS to help them stop in times of overwhelm and consider if they were: Hungry (or hormonal), Angry, Lonely, Tired, or Stressed.

When we can identify what is going on, we are able to keep ourselves from overreacting to situations or being overwhelmed by our feelings, and do something about it instead. Sometimes the solution may be as simple as having some food or drink, taking a quick nap or break if possible, phoning a friend, or connecting with someone to share your feelings.

If we go a step further, we can then learn to recognize patterns. I used to frequently run late in the mornings and would get short and cranky with my kids as they ran around unable to find things, trying to pack their bags. This definitely didn't set a joyous tone for the day, and none of us were happy. I realized that I needed to practice what I was teaching. So, we started getting our things organized the night before, picking out our clothes and packing our bags to be ready for the following morning. Making small changes to our routine dramatically changed the tone of the day.

Whether you need to get more sleep, add in some regular exercise, eat a more balanced diet, get some medical support, or find ways to destress and have fun, when we take practical steps to improve our physical health, it has a flow on effect to how we feel and react. As we care for our bodies and pay attention to their signals we will often find that our joy levels are replenished.

SOUL THIEVES

When I am physically tired, my mind and thinking tend to cascade into a downward spiral, and what wouldn't normally affect me can quickly get out of hand. Our physical bodies, our physiology and biochemistry, are interconnected with our mind and mental health; the two go hand in hand. In many ways, the condition of our soul affects our happiness. If we are wise, we will pay attention to the attitudes and emotions that seek to steal our joy.

Resentment

We used to sing a song in Sunday School that spelled out the word J-O-Y. Essentially, the message was: Jesus first, Yourself last, and Others in between. Growing up in the Salvation Army where we were taught to put others ahead of ourselves, and watching the way in which my mother and grandmother constantly served, these values were indoctrinated into me. *I always had to put others ahead of myself.* But can I just say: This isn't a great way to live. Yes, it's important to put God first, but it says in the Bible that we are to love others as we love ourselves (Matthew 22:39).

For a long time, I didn't love myself. Couple this with a lifetime of always elevating the needs of others above my own, and resentment began to build up. I can tell you firsthand that resentment causes bitterness, leaves us grumpy, and definitely doesn't make us glad! I had to identify the lie that told me I always needed to put myself last, and replace it with the truth that I needed to love others how I love myself. To do this, I first had to learn to love myself; I had to recognize what my needs were, and then balance them with the needs of others. Sometimes, loving ourselves is choosing to say no, putting up boundaries, or limiting time spent doing things that drain you. It can even mean prioritizing your own needs for a season, especially if you are always looking out for others. When we get this biblical balance right, resentment is unable to creep in and steal our joy.

Disappointment

One of the most common joy-thieves is disappointment, and I should know! When the early years of our married life did not turn out as I had expected and we faced constant health challenges and infertility, I was filled with disappointment. Waiting for our dream of having children to be fulfilled was hard, my unmet expectations were a source of grief, and my heart was sick because of it.

I had always thought that when Proverbs 13:12 says, "hope deferred makes the heart sick", it meant that the delay in having children was the thing that made my heart sick, but I have recently come to look at this Scripture in a different way. When *our hope* is deferred, when we no longer have hope for the thing we are waiting for, that's what makes our heart sick.

Due to the lengthy delay we faced in having children, there were times when I lacked hope in this area. I carried sadness with me, and it affected both me and my husband. I wish that I knew then what I know now. I wish that I could have gotten up and shouted for joy, or sung joyful prophetic songs, or asked the God of hope to fill me with all joy and peace as I trusted Him. But because I didn't, disappointment was able to rob me of expectation, and without the hope that God will show us His goodness, it's pretty hard to be joyful.

Lack of Purpose

Proverbs 29:18 tells us that "Where there is no vision, the people perish" (KJV). This was certainly true in my life. A year after I had my daughter, after finally having our dream of a child fulfilled, I found myself rather bored. I am not a natural homemaker, I don't love cooking or baking, I don't do vegetable patches or sewing—they simply don't bring me much satisfaction. Although I was grateful for my life, it seemed mundane and often felt like Groundhog Day.

I talked with my twin sister about how I was feeling and shared that I just didn't really have any vision beyond being a mother. It was a timely conversation, as my sister had just started a Bible study which took participants through the process of writing a vision statement for their life. Over the next four weeks I began to clarify my purpose, identifying my core values, giftings, passions, and the past experiences that had shaped me. Through that study I started to declare that one day I would be a speaker and that I would empower other women to pursue God during difficult times. With this renewed sense of purpose I was able to start taking small steps towards fulfilling this dream, even while being a mother. Again, joy began to return as my understanding of my identity and purpose grew.

Shame

When life was at its most difficult, I remember feeling immense shame. I was deeply embarrassed about how our life was turning out; nothing was as we had expected. Even though none of it was of our doing, I still felt like a failure as a wife. I didn't think anyone would understand my situation so I withdrew and hid away, which only intensified the sadness I felt. Whereas embarrassment is a feeling that resolves with time, shame lies about your identity, affecting your sense of self-worth and causing isolation. These lies need to be addressed so that you can live in the freedom and fullness of joy that Christ intended you to.

Unforgiveness

A number of years ago I was deeply hurt by someone close to me, and after the months of pain and rejection they had put me through, I battled to forgive them. I knew that I *should* forgive, that it was the Christian thing to do, but I didn't want to; I didn't want to let them off the hook too easily. Our conversations, and the arguments as to why I should or should not forgive them, were constantly going around in my head and impacting my moods. I was increasingly cross and angry, and the bitterness was eating me up on the inside. Unforgiveness was stealing my joy.

After a week or so of this internal back and forth tussle, I finally took my struggle to the Lord. Journaling with Him, I let it all out, sharing my hurt and disappointment and my hesitancy to forgive. I held nothing back, no matter how ugly the thought was. I asked Him to show me the truth of the situation, and He spoke gently, showing me what the person involved had been going through and what my friend had been thinking. Through the process He gave me insight and empathy and enabled my heart to shift into alignment with what my head already knew: that I needed to forgive. God's grace empowered me to do what I couldn't do in the natural, and through forgiving, the inner turmoil that was robbing me of peace ceased and joy was able to return.

The Need for Control

Can I ask you a question? *How often do you laugh?* Studies show that generally speaking, adults laugh far less easily and often than most children. But the benefits of laughter are huge—reduced stress, improved mood, relief of pain, increased immunity, and better health and memory, not to mention the enhanced creativity it unleashes.

And yet, it seems that as we grow and enter adulthood, there is this unwritten law, this expectation that we should have it all together and know what we are doing with our lives. We tend to become more serious, especially as we take on the responsibility of parenthood and leadership. One researcher found that one of the biggest restrictions to living wholeheartedly was the desire to look cool and appear to be in control. The problem with this, is that as duty and the need for control take over our lives, they sap us of the capacity for play and laughter.

False Responsibility

Alongside our need for control often comes a false sense of responsibility. We can take things so seriously that we end up carrying a weight we were never intended to, and consequently, our joy in the roles God has entrusted to us gets lost. When I was a young leader, I wanted to be seen to have it all together and was terrified of dropping the ball. I suppose it was about feeling worthy of the position I was in. But as we grow and develop as leaders, why do we still feel the need to continue this perception that we are the experts? Not only is this exhausting, but it can easily lead to pride, like that of the Pharisees.

We need to move back to child-like dependence on Christ, being willing to go out unprepared with just what we have in our hand, just as the disciples were (Matthew 10), and relying not on our planning and effort but on the provision and power of the Holy Spirit. We need to remember that we are not Jesus, and place the burden of responsibility back where it belongs, accepting His invitation to cast our worries and our burdens on Him, knowing He cares deeply for us and for the people we lead and love (1 Peter 5:7).

ATMOSPHERE THIEVES

While many of the things that rob us of joy are internal, some of them are external. During my first year of ministry school, I registered for a class by accident, thinking it was on a different topic—luckily the Lord knew what I needed. The class was called "Shifting Atmospheres" and was about discerning what was going on in the spirit realm. It helped me identify how at times my joy was affected by what others were experiencing rather than my own circumstances. In it, I learnt to determine the spiritual atmosphere and how to shift it.

After the first class, I was wondering what I was doing there. As far as I knew, I had terrible discernment. But little did I know I was highly sensitive to the spiritual realm. Each week the teacher would share what she had been sensing in the spiritual atmosphere, and each week I thought, *I've been feeling that way too*. She taught us about how we can pick up on others' feelings when we walk in a room, and suddenly feel lonely, depressed, or anxious. After so many years of not recognizing that my feelings and emotions are affected by the spiritual atmosphere, I gained freedom and skills from that class I hadn't even planned to attend!

Here are some common 'atmosphere-thieves'. As we learn to discern them, we can shift the heaviness and anxiety we so often carry and bring joy back into the atmosphere!

A Religious Spirit

A religious spirit can affect any area of our life—our home, our workplaces, even our marriages! Often this spirit comes in through a legalistic upbringing, or through a particularly strict church experience. A friend of mine shared recently how in her church growing up, there was a verse printed across the wall at the front of the sanctuary: "Let everything be done decently and in order" (1 Corinthians 14:40 KJV). Imagine how that would stifle freedom! Taken out of context, or at least to an extreme, this verse has been used to stifle and restrict God's people rather than to bring calm to services as was its original intent. When a religious spirit is present, it often uses God's Word, but it opposes the Spirit of God, robbing us of the very joy and freedom Christ came to restore.

A Spirit of Fear

Realistically, how many of our fears are grounded on truth? Even reflecting on the things that I have written about in soul care I can see how I have sanctioned so many lies in my life. These lies have bred resentment, bitterness, shame, isolation, and fear—fear being the ultimate joy-thief.

The enemy loves to sow his lies into our minds, plaguing us with concerns that breed fear and anxiety. He knows that when fear gets in, he holds us captive. Think of what happens when people live in fear—we see control, obsessions, addictions, shame, and 'small living'—the spirit of fear is the ultimate joy-thief!

It is important to remember that *fear is a liar*. In fact, Jesus says of the devil, "There is no truth in him. When he lies, he speaks his native language, for he is a liar and the father of lies" (John 8:44). We must learn to listen instead to the voice of Jesus, who not only speaks the truth (John 8:45); He *is* the truth (John 14:6)! Fear is an oppressive spirit, but the Spirit of God brings freedom and abundance!

A Permissive Spirit

One morning I found that both my husband and I were on edge and irritable at each other. I asked him, "Did you have a dream last night?" to which he replied, "Yes." In his dream, a woman had made advances to him, but Lincoln was quick to reassure me that he had done nothing—my faithful husband didn't want to be seen as unfaithful even in his dreams. I had also had a dream that same night where I was living in a house with a man who wasn't my husband. It had felt disturbing and wrong, and I had woken feeling uncomfortable.

Together we recognized that the shift in atmosphere between us was not due to something either of us had done, and it wasn't physical—it was spiritual. A permissive spirit had sought to divide us, and as soon as we rebuked the enemy, our peace and unity were restored—and our joy returned.

ACTIVATION

Identify one or two things that are stealing your joy, whether they are physical, psychological, or spiritual. If you find there are more, ask the Holy Spirit to help you prioritize how to address them. What are some practical steps you can take to deal with these joy-thieves? Make an action plan for the coming week to put these into practice.

CHAPTER THIRTEEN

Joy, Our Strength

We were filled with laughter, and we sang for joy. And the other nations said, "What amazing things the Lord has done for them."
Psalm 126:2 NLT

We were sitting around our dining room table with our two kids sharing our highs and lows of the day, something we regularly do. Spurred on by a recent encouragement from one of our teachers to include our kids more in our relationship with the Lord, particularly the dreams and prophetic words we receive, I shared the highlight of my day—how the Holy Spirit had filled me with joy and laughter right in our lounge during an online Zoom class. As I started to describe the experience and what God had done, I felt the Holy Spirit's joy rising up within me and began to giggle. The giggle developed into a chuckle and then continued to grow in intensity and volume; I struggled to keep talking, I was laughing so much. As I glanced across at Lincoln not knowing what to do, I saw he was laughing too. But just as quickly, he began to cry, which was the primary way the Holy Spirit had been affecting him in many of his classes.

Our kids looked perplexed. They glanced back and forth from one parent laughing to the other crying and then back at each other, wondering what on earth was going on. Here was their mum, in hysterics slowly sliding off her chair, and their dad with his head on the table quietly weeping. Not knowing what else to do, they continued to eat as we eventually settled down. After we had finished the meal and were cleaning up, my son came up to me and quietly said, "Laugh, Mommy, laugh." We looked at each other and giggled several times. Later that evening when we snuggled up together against his piles of soft toys reading, he asked me to laugh again. "More, Mom, more," he said. I stopped and put the book down and we giggled, laughing freely and about nothing in particular, but oh how we enjoyed it.

Joy is made to be released. It's impossible to be full of joy without it spilling over. And when it does, it brings great strength both to the person releasing it and the one receiving it.

NOURISHED BY JOY

In the book of Nehemiah, we find the often-quoted verse: ". . . the joy of the Lord is your strength" (Nehemiah 8:10). When these words were spoken, the children of Israel had just come out of seventy years of exile, and finally, a portion of the Promised Land had been restored to them. A remnant had returned to Jerusalem to embark on rebuilding the temple, a project that took them four years to complete. Now that the temple was finished, it was time to focus on restoring the city walls. For decades they had tried to secure the walls, but now, through God's miraculous enabling, Nehemiah was able to organize the people to rebuild the walls in just fifty-two days, even with the zealous opposition they faced.

In chapter 8, we find Nehemiah leading a celebration ceremony for the dedication of the new temple. Everyone gathered on the first day of the seventh month, and Nehemiah asked Ezra the priest to read them the Law. The people listened attentively as Ezra read aloud from daybreak till noon, and the other priests joined him in explaining the meaning of what was being said so that everyone had the opportunity to understand. As the Law was read, the people were overcome with grief; they wept as they realized afresh what they had lost living without the Law for so long while they were in exile. But rather than allowing the people to continue in grief, Nehemiah told them three times not to weep or mourn, saying:

> *Go and celebrate with a feast of rich foods and sweet drinks, and share gifts of food with people who have nothing prepared. This is a sacred day before our Lord. Don't be dejected and sad, for the joy of the LORD is your strength!*
> Nehemiah 8:10 NLT

Notice that Nehemiah didn't say it's your repentance or your grief that are your strength, but rather the joy of the Lord! He wasn't saying that repentance wasn't needed, or that there isn't a time for mourning, but that this is not where their strength would be found—it was in joy that they would find their strength! In instructing them to 'eat the fat and drink the sweet', I can't help but wonder if he was giving them a picture of what joy is like to the human spirit. Perhaps in the same way their rich festival food nourished their bodies, joy would nourish their spirits.

But what sort of strength does joy offer us? In this verse, 'strength' is not referring to being made physically strong or capable of resisting force, but refers to a *refuge*, a place or means of safety and protection. God was offering His people *a place to come to* when life was hard and overwhelming.

This invitation couldn't have come at a better time for the Israelites. After having finally completed the rebuilding of the walls, they must have felt emotionally and physically drained. They still had a huge job ahead of them—looking around at the rubble that was once their homes, it must have felt an insurmountable task to rebuild an entire city within those walls. It would have been so easy to feel overwhelmed, to feel defeated before they had even started this next phase, and if they were heavy with their guilt and grief, how much harder that task would have felt. Instead, they were strengthened by the joy of the Lord.

As we read the book of Nehemiah, we discover some keys for how we too can know the refuge and protection that joy offers.

TESTIMONIES AND THANKFULNESS

As the remnant sat around their tables after reading the Law, feasting, and filling up their bellies, I'm sure their hearts were overcome with praise and adoration for their God, who had rescued them from captivity and enabled them to rebuild the temple and city walls. Their thankfulness must have been amplified, having just heard the testimony of what He had done for the generations who came before them. Their resolve would have been strengthened as they pondered how the Lord provided again and again, miraculously dividing the Red Sea, supplying food in the desert and clothes that never wore out; how enemy armies were defeated through worship, and walls came down with a shout. I can just hear the excited chatter across the table and sense the overflow of new joy amongst them as they recounted everything that had been read. Imagine the strength of mind and spirit as they refocused on the goodness of God—how they would have encouraged each other that He would do it again; He would help them rebuild their homes.

There is such power in testimony. Moses knew this when he handed the leadership of the Israelites to Joshua around three hundred years before—it was the reason he instructed Joshua to take time every seven years to remember what God had done (Deuteronomy 31:10-11). If only these instructions weren't lost somewhere along the way, things might have been different for the Israelites. Perhaps they would have remained faithful, finding refuge and strength in thanksgiving, celebration, and rejoicing in the Lord.

When has God come through for you? When have you experienced the good hand of God upon you? What promises has He kept in your life? Tell people about what He has done—share your testimonies with them! Revelation 12:11

(KJV) tells us that "they overcame him (the devil) by the blood of the Lamb and by the word of their testimony." When we speak our God-stories, we are empowered to overcome loss, obstacles and hardships—and so are those who hear them.

But not only must we testify of what God has done, we must also give thanks for it. There's power in gratitude and thankfulness. When our minds are focused on the negative or the difficulties, it's hard to be joyful, but when we give thanks, it shifts our mindset, fills us with hope, and helps us maintain our joy.

INTENDED TO OVERFLOW

The Israelites needed strength of body, mind and spirit for what lay ahead. They had come so far and built so much, but they now needed to rebuild their homes—probably the most difficult and personal task yet. As a community they needed to band together to complete the last stage of the rebuilding of Jerusalem. Nehemiah knew this; he also knew that the only way this could happen was if the poor and the weak in spirit joined in—they needed to be strengthened too. This was why he had encouraged the people not just to go and feed themselves but to also share with those who had none.

There are so many people who need strength, who need the joy of the Lord. Our privilege is that we get to share the choice food and sweet wine that we have; we get to encourage and strengthen others with the joy the Lord has given us.

In the book of Romans, Paul wrote to the church at Rome exhorting them to live a righteous life, and in the latter chapters, he gives them some practical instruction on what this looks like (Romans 14 & 15). Part of this was that they were to look out for the weaker members of the church, who at that stage were the Gentiles. He instructed the stronger members of the congregation not to judge, hurt or offend the weak, but rather to bear with them, accepting and serving them. He concludes with a verse that will now be very familiar to you:

> *May the God of hope fill you with all joy and peace as you trust in him, so that you may overflow with hope by the power of the Holy Spirit.*
> Romans 15:13

The way to support the struggling, the weak, and the hopeless, is to bring joy and peace into their situations, and abound in hope for them. The God of hope, through the power of the Holy Spirit, fills us to overflowing with peace, joy, and hope, not just for ourselves but for others too. Just as the Israelites generously shared their gifts of food with those who had none, we can share our joy. We can overflow with gratitude for what the Lord had done for us, giving testimony to His goodness in our lives. Everywhere we go, we can release hope and peace through the words that we speak—and believe me, people will notice; they will see there is something different about us! If we can stop focusing on and mourning our sin and instead allow His joy to be our strength, the world will get to see the beauty and power of that joy.

The other nations noticed the hand of the Lord on the Israelites; they were known as the chosen people, and it was said among the nations, "the Lord has done great things for them" (Psalm 126:2). I'm not sure if the great things they were talking about was the shift in their circumstances, or whether it was the joy they displayed despite what lay ahead of them—we will never really know. What I do know is that people take note when they see the hand of the Lord upon our lives, regardless of whether our circumstances shift or not, because they see the joy and hope that we carry. This is why joy is potentially the greatest evangelistic tool available to us. It strengthens us and shines with beauty—it will draw the nations to Jesus!

It was a Thursday morning, and I was serving in the online healing rooms with another student. I prayed for people, sharing testimonies of what the

Lord had been doing for me and releasing joy at every possible opportunity, but I could sense the heaviness that my classmate was carrying. Once we had signed off the Zoom call, I inquired about how he was going. He shared his difficulties, how he felt weighed down by depression and PTSD and struggled to watch others being healed and filled with joy and laughter while he watched on.

I listened intently, wanting to be sensitive to his feelings but also wanting to give hope to his heart. After some time, I gently asked if I could pray for him and release my testimony. I shared the grief and pain I had experienced for so long and how I always felt I needed to work at being joyful, but how recently that had all changed. I asked the Lord to minister to him, to fill him with all joy and peace so that he could abound in hope. I then encouraged him to keep asking the Lord for joy, just as I had, reminding him that God wants to give it to us more than we want it.

Several weeks later I saw my new friend in the corridor, and he hurried over towards me. He looked different; his countenance was changed. No longer did he look downtrodden, but instead he radiated hope. "Kyllie, you wouldn't believe it," he exclaimed, "I've got joy! Someone prayed for me the other day in class, and I was filled with joy like never before. I was filled with laughter, and something shifted. I feel different. Thank you so much for your prayers and encouragement."

It has been beautiful to watch this man continue to walk out his healing over the past few years, to see him free of depression and PTSD, and experiencing greater levels of joy. What a privilege to be able to share with others who are in need, to strengthen them with joy, and see God get the glory.

ACTIVATION

For the next week, keep a gratitude journal. Write down your blessings; make a list of the good things in your life. Don't keep the goodness of God to yourself though—purposefully release joy into the atmosphere through testimony and thankfulness. If you have kids, bring them in on this by getting them to identify three or more things that they are thankful for—either at the dinner table, or in the car on the way to school, or whenever works for your family.

CHAPTER FOURTEEN

The Restoring Power of Joy

They will be called oaks of righteousness, a planting of the Lord for the display of his splendor. They will rebuild the ancient ruins and restore the places long devastated; they will renew the ruined cities that have been devastated for generations.
Isaiah 61:3-4

During one of our summer breaks, a couple did some house sitting for us while we went home to New Zealand to catch up with family and friends. When we returned, we found they had left a hummingbird feeder hanging from the pergola and we were thrilled to have regular visits from these small, exquisite birds. They would frequently buzz around, their little wings flapping up to eighty beats a second as they sipped on the sweet nectar and enjoyed the flowers in the garden. It's amazing to think that these small birds migrate up to five hundred miles on their own, relying on their fat stores, which account for up to fifty percent of their body weight, to sustain them.

After several weeks of being home, however, I noticed that these little birds were no longer around. That's when I realized the feeder was empty. The sweet syrup was no longer attracting them to our yard, no longer fueling their humming wings and strengthening them for their pending migration.

Without the nectar, we didn't get to enjoy watching them joyfully flying around the garden.

As it frequently does these days, my mind wandered to the topic of joy. The sweet nectar was much like joy. When it is lacking in our lives and in the church, people are not attracted to us. And when our attractiveness is diminished, we are less able to attract others to Jesus, less able to give them the strength, nourishment and sustenance they need for life's journey.

At the start of my joy journey, I was only thinking about myself. Little did I realize that others would be watching on, and that possessing the joy of the Lord served a much bigger purpose than simply my own healing. Ultimately, it was for others to be restored and rebuilt, for nations to be impacted, and for God to receive the glory in it all.

A DISPLAY OF HIS SPLENDOR

Isaiah 61 is a familiar passage, and one that is quoted to remind us that God can exchange beauty for our ashes, joy for our mourning, and praise for our heaviness. These are all beautiful promises—and ones that we have already explored here together—but seldom have I heard the focus shift to how these gifts extend beyond us as individuals. There is so much more promised in Isaiah 61. Yes, the passage speaks of God bestowing beauty, joy and praise, but that is not the end of the story. When people receive this divine exchange, they also receive a whole new identity! No longer are they known as those who are broken and in mourning. Having received comfort and strength, people speak differently about them. In verses 3-4 we read, "They will be called oaks of righteousness, a planting of the Lord for the display of his splendor."

Those who once were joyless have found joy—now they are known as 'oaks of righteousness.' The oak tree is a magnificent representation of strength, stability, refuge, and shelter. With a deep root system, the oak is able to adapt to many climates and conditions. It can withstand high winds and storms. It can stand the test of time, providing shelter to all who find refuge under its branches, and offering nourishment and strength to those who eat from its fruits.

Take in these words. This is who you are! When you receive the Lord's joy and allow Him to take your mourning, you become an oak of righteousness; the joy of the Lord enables you to grow into a strong, deeply-rooted tree—a display of His splendor.

Who will call you an 'oak of righteousness'? The people who look on your life! The people who see the transformation that has occurred, who see the grief you have endured and how you are still standing, still producing fruit, still possessing joy. People will be astonished at how you have been able to stay the course, and they will see the beauty you carry. It will draw people to you, and you will share the goodness of God.

Not only are God's people called by a new name, but their transformed lives now serve three incredible purposes. They have become those who: rebuild cities, restore the generations, and display the Lord's splendor. The joy we carry as individuals has a ripple effect, extending out geographically and generationally.

But Isaiah 61 has even more to say about these people who have received beauty for ashes, the oil of gladness for mourning and the garment of praise for the spirit of heaviness. They also receive a 'double portion' that attracts the nations to them. In verses 5-7 we read:

> *Strangers will shepherd your flocks; foreigners will work your fields and vineyards. And you will be called priests of the Lord, you will be named ministers of our God. You will feed on the wealth of nations, and in their riches you will boast. Instead of your shame you will receive a double portion, and instead of disgrace you will rejoice in your inheritance. And so you will inherit a double portion in your land, and everlasting joy will be yours.*

Wow, what a promise for us! We not only get the exchange and the honor of displaying God's splendor, but abundance is released into our lives—a 'double portion' that enables us to help rebuild the lives of others, restore our cities and bring hope to future generations. Out of our experience, our testimony, the fruits of our lives, we become 'double-portion ministers' of God! We get to minister out of what we have received, a double portion of joy *and* blessing, into our families, our workplaces and communities, and in our land!

THE DOUBLE PORTION BELONGS TO YOU

The double portion blessing is not just 'prosperity doctrine'—it's a biblical principle found at least six times in Scripture. We find it first mentioned in Deuteronomy 21:17 where the Law of Moses gave the firstborn the right of succession as well as the double portion of inheritance. In other words, the firstborn was given twice as much as the other children.

When the firstborn became the head of the household, he took on the care of any dependent family members, including any unmarried daughters and his mother, if she was still alive. This second portion was not for himself, but gave the eldest the resources to care for his extended family.

When we are adopted into the family of God, we become co-heirs with Jesus. He is the firstborn of all creation, the firstborn from the dead, the One who has pre-eminence—He has the first place in everything (Colossians 1:15,18). In Christ, there are no second-born children, no grandchildren; we are all firstborn sons and daughters. We receive our position *in Him*; we are seated in heavenly places *with Him*, and we are blessed with every spiritual blessing, including joy, *through Him*. You could say we receive *more* than a double portion!

Like the firstborn son who received twice the inheritance, this double portion isn't intended just so we can live life for our own enjoyment; it's to help us restore and rebuild those around us. There's no pressure to perform or carry all the responsibility for this mission, nor do we have to run ourselves dry. Instead, we get to minister out of the overflow, out of the double portion. The double portion ensures we have enough to keep pouring out and caring for our extended family, for our community, for those who are vulnerable and in need. Just as in the story of the widow, there's great capacity for the oil of gladness to continue to flow until every vessel is full—until hearts are restored to the Father, generational blessing is released, and our nations are impacted for Jesus.

A GLOBAL OUTBREAK OF JOY

During the Covid pandemic, people around the world experienced something our generation had never seen before—social distancing, faces hidden behind masks, separation from one another even during the moments in life that usually bring us together. With the loss of jobs, businesses and livelihoods, households and national economies felt increasing financial pressure. Many were overcome with worry for their health and future. If the world *and* the church ever needed to experience an outbreak of joy, it is in our generation. It is *now*.

Imagine if Christians around the world were infected with joy—spilling out, 'leaking down their legs', contagious joy! Imagine the change in countenance, the communities united and transformed, the atmospheres shifting in our personal lives, our families, our churches, and our nation. Picture the smiles, the joyful embracing, the celebration!

I can see it now—people being filled with the joy of the Lord, the chains of addiction falling off, fear and anxiety shifting, depression healed, and grief lifted—people laughing and abounding in hope even for hopeless situations, regaining the ability to dream again. I see the church filled with joyful displays of singing, dancing, and laughing—there's no religious spirits or legalism, only freedom. Salvations multiply as people see our cheerful hearts. They're drawn to the Lord because they want what we have—they want our joy! *Can you see it too? Can you see why joy is the greatest evangelistic tool available?*

Through the power of supernatural joy being poured out upon us, lives will be restored and rebuilt. As they watch us, they will see the splendor of the Lord and give God the glory! But it is not only individuals who will be filled with joy—nations will too! Just as the surrounding nations took notice when Israel was rebuilt, declaring, "The Lord has done great things for them" (Psalm 126:2), so will the nations of our time and in our generation.

∼

I long to hear testimonies of joy, stories of how the Holy Spirit has strengthened people with joy, maturing them into 'oak trees' that offer shelter, sustenance, and refuge to others. There are testimonies yet to be released of the fruit of joy—how generations and cities were changed, and the lands received a double portion. But I don't have those testimonies yet—only time will provide these.

My prayer is that this would be the legacy not only of this book and of my life, but also of yours—that through what I have received from the Lord and given to you, those who are captives of grief will be set free to dance, sing, laugh, and minister out of an overflow of joy. I pray for an endless cycle of joy to be set in motion, until the nations are won for Jesus!

ACTIVATION

1. Picture yourself as an oak of righteousness, one who stands with strength and longevity. Your branches stretch wide, creating shelter for others, and are laden with a double portion of fruit, feeding those who are resting under it. Visualize the lives who are being rebuilt and restored, how they are changed, and the effect for generations to come.

2. Now journal what that could look like—whose life could be impacted, and how? Dream big for your family, for your community and your nation, remembering that God can do immeasurably more than you can ask or imagine. In other words, if you can imagine it, God can do it—and then some!

An Impartation of Joy

I remember the first time I heard a sermon devoted to the topic of joy. I had heard joy spoken of in the context of trials, or the fruit of the Spirit, but this was different—the whole message was about God's abundant, extravagant joy. I was engrossed, writing everything down that I could.

Luckily that day, I just happened to be sitting in the front row of the auditorium, off to the side in front of the stairs leading from the stage. At the end of the sermon, the pastor explained that he wanted to impart joy to us through the laying on of hands. Running off the stage, he came directly towards me and planted his hands on my head. Suddenly I was thrown backwards into my chair. I thought at first that it was just the force of him energetically running off the stage, but as I tried to sit up, I realized I physically couldn't; the power of the Spirit was so heavy upon me. For the next twenty minutes I lay in my chair, unable to move, until my husband, who had delayed our departure as long as possible, came and whispered in my ear, "We're going to be late picking up the kids if we don't go now." With great difficulty, he helped peel me off the chair, and I staggered to the car feeling like I was under a heavy, weighted blanket.

I have hardly any memory of the hours that followed, but the next morning I woke to singing in my mind. I could feel that my joy had increased, and I was aware of a stronger connection with the Holy Spirit. This was the first time that I had experienced an impartation through the laying on of hands.

I can't physically lay hands on you to impart what I have received, but I have laid my hands on this keyboard, pouring out my story and sharing my life with you. Now, in the spirit, I lay my hands upon you and speak these words of impartation, over you, my readers:

I raise my flask over your head and pour out the oil of joy. Here, in the Father's presence, I declare that fullness of joy abounds. As He releases rejoicing over you, I raise my voice in agreement. I declare that Zion is your native home! Songs of joy surround you, and gladness overtakes you. Gone are the days of sowing in tears—the time has come for you to reap with joy.

I release a shout of triumph over you. Grief is conquered, the enemy is destroyed. Your chains have fallen off! Walk out of captivity and into the joy of the Lord. A double portion is your inheritance! You have joy enough to sustain your family, your church, your nation! I bless you with all joy.

You have become a display of His splendor!

Author's Note

While writing the last few chapters of this book, I found myself feeling the pressure to get everything out on the page and make my deadlines. After writing for so many months, my words were depleted, and I was struggling to express my thoughts. I could feel my joy diminishing as a result. I didn't want to finish writing out of duty; I wanted to complete it full of joy. So, I took a writing break, and spent time with the Lord to refresh. As I did, God gave me more than what I asked for—He gave me a *double portion* of joy. Time and time again during worship, I experienced His presence come upon me and fill me with more joy. At times it even felt like I couldn't take much more—I was full to overflowing. I would wake with joy on my mind and a song in my heart. All I wanted to do was share the Lord's goodness with others, to lay hands on and pray for them, releasing joy, sharing the double portion God had poured out over me. I realized I had come full circle.

My hope as you finish this book is that you don't leave with just a set of tools, but that you would leave with a greater revelation of the *person* of joy—that through learning to behold, to abide, and to 'yada', you have grown in greater intimacy with the Lord. As you continue to activate these concepts in your life, do so in connection with the Holy Spirit. Allow Him to teach you and to guide you as to what to use and when. At times you will feel led to sit and lament with the Lord; other times He may want you to shout in triumph declaring the battle is already won, or to get up and sing prophetically. Sometimes He may simply invite you to stand strong and remember what the Lord has done. Be sensitive to these promptings—He knows what you need.

For those of you who have long-term conditions or unchanging circumstances, I want to encourage you. In many ways I understand what you are going through. Although I wasn't living with the pain myself, I was living with the fear, worry, stress, and the financial and physical impact on my family's life, as well as the disappointment of not yet seeing the miracle. I know that it's tough, and my heart goes out to you. I don't understand why some get breakthrough and others don't; there are answers we will only know when we get to heaven, and some mysteries we have to live with for now. But what I do know is that God is good, and He is steadfast and faithful.

When the Apostle Paul was afflicted, the Lord said to him, "My grace is sufficient for you, for my power is made perfect in your weakness" (2 Corinthians 12:9). This word 'grace' means 'that which affords joy, pleasure, delight, and sweetness'. God affords and provides joy and delight for *you*. His joy is sufficient for *you*; He is sufficient for *you*—not in a minimalist sense, as in, just enough, but His joy is sufficient in all circumstances and fully satisfies. This is His promise to you.

Paul said "I have learnt the secret of being content in any and every situation, whether well fed or hungry, whether living in plenty or in want. I can do all this through him who gives me strength" (Philippians 4:12-13). I wonder if this secret to contentment, the thing that gave him strength despite the thorn in his flesh, was, in fact, the joy of the Lord enabling him to be content despite his situation, to celebrate amidst trials, and to encourage others to rejoice always.

I know that we don't often see this, and most people haven't experienced it yet, but what if what the Bible promises is actually possible? What if contentment in every situation is attainable through supernatural joy? Let's change our beliefs, increase our expectation, and let a different experience be the fruit!

AN IMPARTATION OF JOY

If you do not yet feel like you are in a place where you can believe for more, I release hope over you. I urge you to declare the words of Isaiah 35:1-2 with me:

> *The desert and the parched land* **will** *be glad; the wilderness* **will** *rejoice and blossom. Like the crocus, it* **will** *burst into bloom; it* **will** *rejoice greatly and shout for joy.*

I encourage you to continue speaking these words over yourself. Pray and prophecy what is promised. Out of the desert you *will* blossom again; you *will* rejoice and shout for joy. More joy *will* come.

Acknowledgements

The biggest thank you to my soul-mate, my love, **my supportive husband, Lincoln**. Appreciate. (inside joke). You have always believed in me and encouraged me to reach for my dreams. Thank you for being my partner through the ups and the downs of life. I wouldn't have wanted to do it with anyone else. Thank you for giving me the support, the space, the time and resources to write. For all those lonely nights when I was writing and those times when I was quietly pondering inside my head, those times when I seemed more married to this book than you . . . love you much. Cheer, Bro.

To my children, Pieta and Flynn. You have taught me so much about how to live life, how to have fun, and how to laugh. Pieta, you brought us such light during a dark time, and you still do. You have such a kind and generous heart, always thinking of others. Flynn, you brought exuberance into our quiet family and express your love so generously. I love you both more than words can say.

To my mum, Margaret, and my late father, Peter. You instilled into me a love for the Lord and for others, through both word and deed. Mum, thank you for showing me how to serve, considering others on the fringes. Dad, thank you for demonstrating what it is to dream big with God and work hard to fulfill those dreams. To my brothers, Julian and Lyndon, thank you for continuing the legacy of our parents. Without your dedication I wouldn't be able to do what I am doing now.

To my twin sister, Janelle. Thank you for your close attention to detail, your ideas for marketing, and for always asking the hard questions others don't, even when it seems harsh. I'm so grateful for all the ways you love me and want me to thrive.

To Chris and Janette. Thank you for welcoming me into your family and sharing the joy of your son with me. Thank you for your acceptance, your love, your support, and all your acts of service, especially through those difficult years—the house decorating, the spouting, the moving, the cooking and baking (and especially those twelve-egg, triple level chocolate cakes with the world's best ganache). I wish I could have had one for my book launch—none of it ever went unnoticed.

To my girl posy: my sunshine girls, women's group, Mint Friday, the Shinecity team, my prayer support, soundboards, cheerleaders, encouragers, my long-term friends and newer ones. I have been so blessed to have you all in my life. I used to teach in the ShineWomen course that diamonds can only be cut and shaped by other diamonds. I am so lucky to have rubbed shoulders with so many stunning diamonds who have helped shape me into the woman of God that I am. I am eternally blessed.

To Carmel and Jason and the members of Clifflife Church. Thank you for seeing something in me and giving me a platform to learn and grow. For supporting us to follow the Lord's calling, sending us out and welcoming us back with open arms, thank you.

To Yvonne and Andy. Thank you for the early editing and encouragement. You gave me confidence that this story was worth writing.

To Anya McKee and the editorial team at Torn Curtain Publishing. This book would not look or read like it does today without your tireless efforts at editing and your attention to detail. I know you gave it extra time and attention because it needed it and you believed in the message. Anya, thank you for your affirmation, your wisdom, and your prayers. I couldn't have wished for a better mentor for writing my first book. You started as my editor and finished as my friend. It was fun, let's do it again.

To Bridget and Jeremy Hilliard, my third-year mentors, and the wider Bethel Leaders Network team who have supported me in the final stages of bringing this message to the world. You instilled so much confidence in me and helped me believe that I am a big leader with lots to share. You have my deepest gratitude.

To the Bethel School of Supernatural Ministry staff and all the students who went on this journey with me, a special thanks. Many of you have been mentioned throughout this book, and there are many more who have taught me about the joy of the Lord. You will find so much of your teachings illustrated and echoed in these words. You probably deserve some of the royalties! Thank you for demonstrating to me that greater levels of joy are available, for changing my life by how you each live yours, for showing me that there is nothing more important than God's presence and power and that we owe the world an encounter with Him. I am forever grateful for the impact you have made into my and my family's lives. We will never be the same.

Lastly and most importantly, I want to thank **my faithful God**. This book would not have been possible without encountering You personally. Thank You for Your divine revelation through the Holy Spirit. You are truly the Teacher, the Author and Finisher.

If you have experienced a fresh encounter while reading this book, I would love to hear about it! You can get in touch with me at:

www.KyllieMartin.com

You will go out in joy and be led forth in peace; the mountains and hills will burst into song before you, and all the trees of the field will clap their hands.
Isaiah 55:12

www.ingramcontent.com/pod-product-compliance
Lightning Source LLC
Chambersburg PA
CBHW051437290426
44109CB00016B/1591